Steve Biko

by Wilson

OHIO UNIVERSITY PRESS
ATHENS

Ohio University Press, Athens, Ohio 45701
www.ohioswallow.com
All rights reserved

First published in 2011 by Jacana Media (Pty) Ltd
10 Orange Street, Sunnyside
Auckland Park 2092
South Africa
(+29 11) 628-3200
www.jacana.co.za

To obtain permission to quote, reprint, or otherwise reproduce or distribute
material from Ohio University Press publications, please contact our rights
and permissions department at (740) 593-1154 or (740) 593-4536 (fax).

First published in North America in 2012 by Ohio University Press
Printed in the United States of America
Ohio University Press books are printed on acid-free paper ⊗ ™

20 19 18 17 16 15 14 13 12   5 4 3 2 1

ISBN: 978-0-8214-2025-6
e-ISBN: 978-0-8214-4441-2

Library of Congress Cataloging-in-Publication Data

Wilson, Lindy.
  Steve Biko / Lindy Wilson.
      p. cm. — (Ohio short histories of Africa)
  "First published in 2011 by Jacana Media, Auckland Park, South Africa."
  Includes bibliographical references and index.
  ISBN 978-0-8214-2025-6 (pb : alk. paper) — ISBN 978-0-8214-4441-2
(electronic)
  1. Biko, Steve, 1946–1977. 2. Political activists—South Africa. 3. South
Africa—History—1961–1994. 4. South Africa—Race relations. 5. South
Africa—Politics and government—1994– I. Title. II. Series: Ohio short
histories of Africa.
  DT779.8.B48W55 2012
  968.06092—dc23
  [B]
                                2012020802

Cover design by Joey Hi-Fi

Photo credits: Steve Biko Foundation, p. 21; *Daily Dispatch*, pp. 9, 58, 66, 107, 121,
127, 134, 140 (with thanks as well to Wendy Woods); Bruce Haigh, p. 127; UWC
Robben Island Mayibuye Centre, p. 51; UCT Library, p. 74; Historical Papers,
Wits University Library, p. 37 (bottom left); Bailey's African History Archive, pp.
37 (top), 146; National Archives, p. 43; Benjamin Pogrund, p. 37 (bottom right);
Peter Bruce, p. 154; John Reader/*Life Magazine* © Time, Inc.: p. 39.

Contents

Preface 7

1. Introduction 11
2. Early years, 1946–1965 18
3. Student action and style of leadership,
   1966–1972 30
4. To love and to work 54
5. Bantu – Son of Man, 1973–1977 76
6. Choices and dilemmas 112
7. Detention, banishment and international
   engagement 118
8. Arrest 129
9. A life still to be 'dug out'. 143

Bibliography 155
Index 158

Preface

This brief biography of Bantu Stephen Biko is grounded in relevant published literature. Much written evidence has been lost, was deliberately destroyed or carefully not recorded, out of fear of reprisals in a fearful age. Thus Biko's story draws substantially from interviews. Some were done with Biko himself, particularly near the end of his life. Twenty-six were conducted in 1989 and 1990 before the end of apartheid. Interviews, of course, have weaknesses as historical sources. They are subjective and also rely on memory, often blurred and distorted by time and perspective. Further, describing another's life is sometimes a projection of one's own.

An earlier version of this biography was published in 1991 as a chapter in the book *Bounds of Possibility*. It was written at the invitation of Barney Pityana, Malusi Mpumlwana and Mamphela Ramphele, the co-editors of the book, who have kindly agreed to my revising it for publication in this form.

1

Introduction

September '77
In Port Elizabeth weather fine
It was business as usual
In Police Room 619
       – 'Biko', by Peter Gabriel

On 12 September 1977 'business as usual' for the South African Security Police claimed the life of Bantu Stephen Biko, the twenty-first person to die in a South African prison within a period of twelve months. Biko was 30 years old.

Ten days earlier Biko was reported to be physically sound when visited by a magistrate at the Walmer police cells in Port Elizabeth. He did, however, request 'water and soap to wash himself and a washcloth and a comb', and added: 'I want to be allowed to buy food. I live on bread only here. Is it compulsory that I have to be naked? I have been naked since I came here.'

On the morning of 6 September, Biko faced a

team of Security Police in Room 619 of the Sanlam Building under the leadership of Maj. Harold Snyman, appointed to interrogate 'the Black Power detainees'. According to evidence given to the Truth and Reconciliation Commission by Det.-Sgt. Gideon Nieuwoudt at his amnesty hearing in 1998, Biko sat down on a chair facing his interrogator, Capt. Daantjie Siebert, who immediately ordered him to stand. Later, when Biko sat down again, Siebert grabbed him by the chest and yanked him to his feet. Nieuwoudt asserts that 'Biko pushed the chair forward and lunged with his fist'. Five men then assaulted him simultaneously, 'Blows were aimed backwards and forwards', which also flung him against the walls of the narrow room. Nieuwoudt thrashed him with a reinforced hosepipe. 'In the momentum', he said, 'Mr Biko hit his head, fell, seemed confused and dazed … Siebert then told me to chain him to the [horizontal] bars of the security gate with arms outstretched [at shoulder height] … two sets of hand-cuffs and leg irons also attached – standing.' He was left in this crucifying position for six hours, only able to move his head. Three to four hours later, when Biko asked for water his words were incoherent as if 'under the influence of liquor', Nieuwoudt went on to testify.

That night Biko was left lying on a urine-wet mat, still shackled by leg-irons on his feet which were locked

12

onto the walls. Although Lt.-Col. P.J. Goosen, Officer Commanding, Eastern Cape Security Police, spoke at the inquest into Biko's death about his suspicion at the time that Biko had 'suffered a stroke' and said he had called in a doctor, Nieuwoudt reported at the TRC hearing that the first doctor only appeared 24 hours after the injury and to no effect, leaving Biko shackled in leg-irons and handcuffs for another night. On 11 September, though specialist evidence indicated brain damage, medical approval was given for him to be driven (naked) in the back of a Landrover hundreds of kilometres to Pretoria, where he died from the head injuries he had earlier sustained.

The details of Biko's death horrified the world.

In spite of the inquest that followed, in which the doctors and police displayed a measure of callousness so shocking that their evidence would be transcribed, virtually word for word, into a theatrical performance for audiences world-wide to witness, the details of what actually happened still remain shrouded. None of the Security Police who applied for amnesty from the TRC in 1998 was granted it. The requirement was to tell the *whole* truth. This 'we may never know', commented chairperson George Bizos.

It is, however, Biko's life-giving force that concerns us here. His vitality drew people to him, not only for his sharp intelligence and generous counsel but for his exuberant energy and contagious laugh; not only for his clear thinking and his refreshing political insight but for his capacity to listen, his ability to place himself within a circle of people and not position himself up-front. Biko's gift of leadership was not that people should follow him in a slavish kind of way but that, suddenly, and to their great surprise, they discovered *themselves* and empowered themselves with their own resources.

Basically, Biko was appalled at what he saw all around him in South Africa at the time: 'the black man has become a shell, a shadow of man … bearing the yoke of oppression with sheepish timidity,' he said. He challenged blacks not to be a part of their own oppression, believing that 'the most potent weapon in the hands of the oppressor is the mind of the oppressed'. He defined Black Consciousness as 'an inward-looking process' to 'infuse people with pride and dignity'. 'We have set out on a quest for a true humanity,' he said clearly.

Young as he was, he realised that a new psychological climate had to be created if the liberation of his country was to come about. He expressed what he saw as the bitter truth. Of prime importance was 'to awaken the people as to who they are by getting them to state their identity. He thought that if you could do that, then there was no stopping them from revolution,' explained his colleague Malusi Mpumlwana.

This consciousness towards a realised identity, a refusal to mirror white apartheid's definition of black inferiority, gradually took root amongst the black youth and revived political energy in the 1970s. A new dignity and a refusal to be afraid helped fuel those in emerging trade unions; it gave determination to the many working in grassroots organisations; it empowered lawyers, doctors, priests, poets, mothers and fathers. Its youthful followers, scattered by the apartheid regime especially after 1976, later joined and vitalised new thinking in the ranks of the banned, imprisoned and exiled liberation movements of the African National Congress (ANC) and the Pan Africanist Congress (PAC).

Biko's life expressed in words only, diminishes him. His arrival in the doorway, his large physical frame relaxed into a chair, were essential elements of who he was. The welcome he gave, the sound of his laughter and his immediate questioning curiosity are glaringly missing here. He is not easily packaged. Biko was by no means a paragon of virtue. Though he could hold his drink, he often drank too much; he earned a reputation of being a 'womaniser'; and he could not always judge for himself his own emotional and psychological capacity. He was essentially human but also exceptional. Biko strongly criticised the institutional Church yet he believed in God and had insight into Christ's teachings. He was not a Marxist – indeed he was much criticised for this – identifying more with what his close friend Barney Pityana refers to as the 'Hegelian thesis–antithesis'. He believed in bargaining from a position of strength, as witnessed in the Saso-BPC Trial, where Biko stated in public: 'We certainly don't envisage failure … We have analysed history … the logical direction is that eventually any white society in this country is going to have to accommodate black thinking. We are mere agents in that history.'

Pityana would argue that Biko's historical analysis lacked the force of Marxist historical materialism. Biko regarded the common oppression of all blacks as being a stronger political motive for change, and more unifying, than that of class; he recognised that to forge a powerful identity among the majority would potentially shift political power. He was more at home in African socialism than in socio-political examples from Europe.

Although he set out to study medicine he never became a doctor. Although he never had time to complete his law studies, he donned the mantle of a lawyer of considerable skill when summoned to give evidence in defence of those in the organisations he helped establish. And although he never set out to become a martyr, this is what he became. Perhaps the thing he least set out to do was to convert white South Africans, yet the Black Consciousness Movement jolted white youth into a profound self-examination that changed the political direction of a whole generation; and he converted one of the leading liberal newspaper editors without apparent effort. Above all, although he advocated a philosophy called 'Black Consciousness', Steve Biko was not a racist.

This brief narrative of his life traces some of the origins of Biko's political thinking and the role he played in connecting Black Consciousness and self-identity. It reveals his innate curiosity and fascination with the human condition, with humanity, with what being human truly is, particularly in Africa.

2

Early years, 1946–1965

Bantu Stephen Biko was born on 18 December 1946 in Tarkastad, in the Eastern Cape, the third child of Mzingaye and Alice Nokuzola 'Mamcethe' Biko. His birth, in his grandmother's home, included the traditional smearing and burying of the umbilical cord into the floor of the room where he was born. Mzingaye chose to name him Bantu Stephen Biko. 'Bantu' literally means 'people'. Later Biko called himself 'son of man'. Although this was done often with tongue in cheek, Malusi Mpumlwana interprets Biko as understanding his name to mean that he was a person for other people or, more precisely, *umntu ngumtu ngabanye abantu*, 'a person is a person by means of other people'.

The name Stephen was prophetic of the manner of his death. It connects with that of his biblical namesake, Stephen, who was stoned to death. Stephen accused the Jews of being false to their vocation, of being stubborn, like their forebears, in refusing to acknowledge that truth. Mpumlwana adds: 'Jesus was actually the path of the Truth, which is very much in line with what the whole vocation of Israel was about. Even as he died he challenged them in the face of their anger.' Stephen Biko challenged people to recognise their humanity and acknowledge it. This included the authorities and those who persecuted him. But they could not see him as a human being nor recognise who he was. They, too, were bound to kill him.

Biko grew up in a Christian family. His parents met and married in Whittlesea when Mzingaye was sent to work with Mamcethe's father, both of them policemen. The Bikos were later transferred to Queenstown, then to Port Elizabeth, to Fort Cox and finally King William's Town, where they lived in a house in the black location of Ginsberg. In 1950, when Mzingaye was studying for a law degree by correspondence through the University of South Africa (Unisa), he fell ill. After being admitted to St Matthew's Hospital in Keiskammahoek, he died. Biko (who was called Bantu by his family) was 4 years old. The first-born, his sister Bukelwa, had been delegated by her father to look after him, while Khaya, an elder brother, was to look after his younger sister, Nobandile. Though the children kept asking where their father was, Mamcethe could not at first bring herself to tell them he had died. Because he was often away, she said he had gone to Cape Town for work and an aeroplane would bring him back. While playing with a group of other children they saw an aeroplane and shouted: 'Aeroplane, come back with our father!' But the other children said: 'No, your father died!'

As a widow with four young children, Mamcethe earned a meagre income for the next 23 years as a domestic worker. She remembers her first employer, the superintendent of Ginsberg, as a helpful and 'good man', who welcomed her children to play with his, included them at Christmas time and was generally generous. After he left, she had to take a job as a cook in the much tougher environment of Grey Hospital in King William's Town, the 'whites-only' town across the railway line from Ginsberg location.

Ginsberg was a closely knit community of about eight hundred families, every four families sharing communal taps and toilets. In spite of her slender means, Mamcethe's house, though simple, was by no means destitute, and with her quiet and singular dignity she always welcomed her friends and neighbours. 'Everybody knew the next person,' Biko's younger sister Nobandile remembers. 'It was common, then, if you didn't have food, you'd go to your neighbours and they'd give you samp, beans, mealie meal, sugar in dishes, and when you had [eaten] you'd just return the dishes.' Biko and Nobandile grew up side by side in the small township, where the languages of English,

Nobandile Biko.

Alice Nokuzola 'Mamcethe' Biko.

Khaya Biko.

Bukelwa Biko.

Afrikaans and Xhosa intermingled. At the age of 6 or 7 he took Nobandile, aged 4, to the creche each day on his way to Charles Morgan Primary School and collected her on his way home.

From a young age Biko made people laugh, not only by tomfoolery and clowning but by the way he engaged in conversation. If he had been too busy playing soccer in the streets and had missed a meal, he would demand it with the next one. He avoided doing things that bored him: errands for aunts or feeding the chickens before school, when he would deliberately get up late. He loved experiments and, like most boys, used his younger sister as guinea pig, but Nobandile 'enjoyed every minute' of that shared childhood with him and, on reflection, remembers that 'We never regarded ourselves as poor though when I look back I realise that, in fact, we were poor'.

Soon, tall and slender, the youthful Biko went off to secondary school at Forbes Grant. His mother began to notice that when other children had parties he refused to have clothes bought for him and he would say: 'I know we don't have a father. We can't afford these new clothes.' Though she would tell him not to worry about such things, the truth is that he worried about his mother all his life. He was deeply committed to her well-being. It made a profound impression on him that she laboured for such long hours in such unrewarding jobs, for very little pay.

Mamcethe wanted her children to be educated. Biko was doing so well at school that the Ginsberg community gave him a bursary to go to Lovedale Institution in nearby Alice, where his brother, Khaya, was already in boarding school. The bursary was, in fact, from money collected to build two senior classrooms, which had not materialised. Biko was 16. Within the first three months of his arrival, Khaya was arrested, suspected of sympathies with the banned PAC. Biko was arrested too. 'They took us to the police camp, decided I was the younger of the two and sent me in first for a sort of heavy grilling, seven people around me. It didn't take long for them to discover that I didn't know a single thing about it. They were talking about "friends" of mine who had been arrested; I didn't know these people. They were talking about things I was *doing* with "friends"; I didn't know about this. This was how I got a glimpse into what was going to happen to my brother. I never saw him thereafter. He just disappeared. I saw him ten months later. It was a bitter experience. I was terribly young.' Khaya was convicted but acquitted on appeal. When Biko returned to Lovedale school, he was immediately expelled although he was entirely innocent. 'I began to develop an attitude which was much more directed at authority than at anything else. I hated authority like hell.'

In 1964, having missed a full year of studies, Biko went to boarding school at St Francis College in Mariannhill, outside Durban. He had just turned 18. It was run by Catholic nuns and monks, and he later described an atmosphere free of government intervention. 'I think it helped a lot in the formulation of ideas in a slow sense. We saw the principal and all the authorities [as] obviously not representative of the system but, all the same, they had an approach to us which was sort of provocative and challenging. That's where one began to see, in a sense, the totality of white power. These were liberals, presumably, who were enunciating a solution for us.' Biko was not loath to question anybody and did so: 'I personally had many wars with those guys, most of them non-political wars in a sense, but again this kind of authority problem.'

Biko began to question 'all sorts of [practices] within the Church, within the authority structure within the school'. He befriended a Catholic nun, who gave him a good deal of her time discussing such issues as the position of nuns within the Church, for example, and why it was necessary to have the institution anyway, which apart from other things imposed strictly disciplined relationships between nuns and monks. And, doubtless, he was curious about celibacy. He also sought answers to these questions by initiating a correspondence with Father Aelred Stubbs, of the Anglican Community of the Resurrection, who was principal of St Peter's College at the Federal Theological Seminary in Alice. Father Stubbs had, in his normal round of duty, come across the Biko family at the time of the two boys' arrest. It was the start of an important and long-term relationship between spiritual 'father' and 'son'.

As we shall see later when Biko befriended a challenging young Anglican priest, David Russell, he would continue to pursue with interest questions of faith and belief, his understanding of religion and his disappointment in the Church. Consciously, however, these questions were not central to his life. Already, at school in Mariannhill, he sought information of an increasingly political nature and he recalled how the pupils found intellectual debates valuable, particularly about Africa's independence from colonialism, which was then under way: 'We were great listeners to news services,' Biko recalled, 'and at that time [Hastings] Banda [of Malawi] and a whole host of other African leaders were coming up.' Several of them became 'heroes', particularly Algeria's Ahmed Ben Bella. Biko himself identified particularly with Oginga Odinga, one of Kenya's national leaders. Their ideas and stances were hotly debated while the whole question of military coups was carefully discussed. Biko remembered, however, that all of them agreed on the idea of a common society. 'I don't know to what extent Christian principles played a part here,' he mused, 'but I was always sold on the idea of a common society.' He added that nobody could enunciate the method or approach or design on his behalf but that, talking of himself as an 'oppressed person', he would do so for himself.

Biko was full of zest and youthful confidence whenever he came home. He would arrive at the door in high spirits, hardly pausing before describing his journey home and everyone he had met. 'He was like a father who comes home. We would hug and kiss and there would be laughter,' Nobandile recalls, and then the two of them might go off the next day and visit some of the older, more lonely people in the township, or they would sit on the verandah until late at night singing Gibson Kente songs. It was partly this zest for life, combined with incorrigible optimism and excitement at Africa's increasing independence, that drew him towards the future rather than the pessimism of the immediate present.

He had been only a boy of 13 when the protest against the carrying of passes took place with the subsequent massacre at Sharpeville in 1960 and both the major black political movements, the ANC and PAC, were banned and went underground. Spurred by the police action at Sharpeville, which killed 69 people in that non-violent protest, there was strong opinion in both organisations that the door had finally closed on passive resistance and that some form of insurgency was necessary for fundamental change in South Africa. Biko was 14 when Nelson Mandela proposed, in June 1961, the formation of the military wing of the ANC, Umkhonto weSizwe (MK). He was 15 when Mandela was arrested on his return from an illegal visit overseas and sentenced to five years' imprisonment, and he was 16 when most of the MK national high command were arrested at Liliesleaf Farm in Johannesburg (he himself also being arrested at Lovedale) and were sentenced to life imprisonment after the Rivonia Trial in 1964.

Running alongside the ANC's 'controlled sabotage' programme was the PAC's militant group, known as Poqo. It was with this organisation that his brother Khaya had been suspected of having connections. Biko talks of the only 'politicos' in his family being PAC and how 'at a very young age I listened to a whole host of their debates'. The PAC was not sympathetic towards Communist ideology nor did it readily accept white membership at that stage. In spite of his admiration for their courage and their 'terribly good organisation', Biko was not convinced by what he saw as an exclusive Africanism.

When Steve Biko matriculated from school in 1965, aged 19, all this history had only very recently come to pass. As far as the government was concerned, the black opposition was neatly rolled up into jails under lock and key or had fled into exile. To what extent all these events were known or in what way they affected the emergent ideas of the young Biko is difficult to judge. Whatever the case, Biko soon expressed his distaste at what he saw as 'this sort of appalling silence on the part of Africans and this tendency to play kids and hide behind the skirts of white liberals who were speaking for them'. Seemingly unscathed and certainly unafraid, Biko believed that blacks could be playing a far greater role. Possibly influenced by his Catholic school background, he believed, at that stage, in what was then known as the 'non-racial' approach – that already established institutions should be opened up to a far greater participation by blacks. Better recruitment and greater numbers of black students would mean that these institutions would shift from being predominantly white to becoming more representative.

Biko wanted to study law at university but there was a popular mentality in the Eastern Cape that equated law with political activism, and was therefore to be discouraged. Medicine was the safe alternative for a good profession, and Biko won a scholarship to study it. There was also a common pattern at the time that bright black students with good matric results should go to the medical school at the University of Natal

(Non-European Section, or UNNE), one of the few possibilities for good tertiary education. Thus many intelligent and remarkable young black students, for whom medicine was not necessarily their first choice, found themselves there in a core group with a measure of freedom which did not exist in any other long-established liberal university, where blacks were always a very small minority.

3

Student action and style of leadership, 1966–1972

In 1966 Biko went to UNNE at Wentworth in Durban to study medicine. He entered the university keen for debate and participation in student politics. In his first year he went as an observer to the July congress of the National Union of South African Students (Nusas), in spite of the many black student groups who disagreed with this decision and with his view of the non-racial approach. In the following year, 1967, he went as a delegate to the congress held at Rhodes University in Grahamstown. Biko immediately challenged Nusas to take an active stance against the segregated residential facilities which Rhodes University had imposed on the congress: those classified as 'Indians' and 'Coloureds' were to stay in the town whilst Africans were required to stay some distance away in a church hall in the 'location'; whites, on the other hand, could stay in the university residences. At the outset of the conference the executive of Nusas dealt with this by bringing in a resolution condemning the Rhodes University Council for not allowing blacks into the residences. Biko then moved a private motion proposing that the conference adjourn until they could find a 'non-racist venue'.

He later remembered that it was during the subsequent debate, which lasted throughout the night, that a lot of ideas became clear to him. 'I realised that for a long time I had been holding onto the whole dogma of non-racism almost like a religion, feeling that it was sacrilegious to question it … I began to feel there was a lot lacking in the proponents of the non-racist idea … They had this problem, you know, of superiority, and they tended to take us for granted and wanted us to accept things that were second-class.'

There was also the assumption that all affairs were automatically conducted in English. This gave an immediate disadvantage to those for whom English was not their mother tongue. It was an extraordinary experience for blacks to listen to their own lives being articulated by whites, who had had an infinitely superior education, yet had had no experience of the reality of being black. Biko recalls the effect: 'You are forced into a subservient role of having to say "yes" to what they are saying because you cannot express it so well. This in a sense [also] inculcates a sense of inadequacy. You tend to think it is not just a matter of language. You tend to tie it up also with intelligence. You tend to feel that that guy is better equipped than you mentally.' Biko identified and experienced, at first hand, the kind of mental process that led to an inferiority complex among blacks. He was certainly not going to succumb to this.

There stirred within him the germ of an idea, which was to flower into a student movement. It conscientised blacks into analysing their socio-political condition by recognising that they could be their own liberators by resisting their oppression with a different mental attitude. It was this mental attitude that became known as 'Black Consciousness'. Amongst other things it debunked long-standing myths whites had woven about Africa generally and South Africa in particular, myths present in school and university textbooks: the inherent inferiority of blacks, their skin-deep civilisation, the simplistic quality of their faith and beliefs, the inferiority of Africa's oral tradition as opposed to written history, the 'primitive' nature of its culture, and so forth. Blacks would be re-conscientised into discovering their true identity by refusing to live the lie. In the spirit of the 1960s world-wide, with the end to colonial rule in Africa, the emergence of Black Power in the United States, and the student revolts in Europe, the Black Consciousness Movement emerged to transform the minds of black South African students, thereby generating a lifestyle which eventually resisted oppression on a massive scale.

On leaving the Nusas meeting Biko went immediately to New Brighton, in Port Elizabeth, to talk to Barney Pityana, who remembers how 'We literally sat in my room for probably the whole night and he was talking through his annoyance and what I was saying to myself was: "Why did you go? You must have known before you went that it would be like that, that nothing is really different and if you did go, you were naive to have expected anything different."'

Pityana had also been dismissed from Lovedale school following a student strike in 1964. He was now one of the leading students in the Anglican Student Society, the English Dramatic Society and the Law Society at the University of Fort Hare. He was not a person easily convinced. He tested and questioned ideas with a legalistic mind: Why this? Why that? Why not the other? Not so much a devil's advocate, he was a person whose intelligence was to be thoroughly trusted and whose questions often brought out aspects not yet considered. In this instance Biko and Pityana were at one and began to work as a convincing team together. Pityana found Biko's idealism attractive. 'There was something about him that was really prepared to experiment with ideas, to really get going, could really take you away from the ordinary humdrum things and say there are other possibilities. He had the capacity to challenge and to make it a reality.'

In July 1968, Pityana and Biko attended a student meeting in Stutterheim of the University Christian Movement (UCM), a newly emerging radical ecumenical group of young people, using the Gospel to challenge the churches to take a more practical, robust approach to counter apartheid and participate to a far greater degree in social change. Under a provision of the Group Areas Act, blacks were allowed to be in any urban area only for 72 hours without a permit. The black participants met to discuss what to do about this. They presented a motion refusing to obey the rule. White delegates expressed displeasure at being left out, and a compromise motion was adopted whereby the whole conference was to march to the borders of the magisterial district. The black caucus also took a formal decision 'to work towards a conference in December to deal with the specific issue of a black student organisation as such'.

Pityana was not convinced about an on-going blacks-only caucus. In a country dominated by segregation, it might easily be seen as a group of students 'taken over by government-orientated thinking'. Shortly afterwards, he invited Biko to speak at Fort Hare at a UCM student discussion to put his point of view. When Biko told students that their responsibility was to the whole university, 'including the people that are working, underpaid, and treated like slaves', Pityana was convinced and saw the potential of the idea as 'a real link between student responsibility and the social concerns of the country'.

Pityana played a leading student role at Fort Hare and, at that time, was determined no Student Representative Council (SRC) should be formed that would be seen to collaborate with the pro-government appointees now ruling the university. In 1968 he was expelled during a strike. As regional director of the UCM, which was not allowed to operate on the Fort Hare campus, Pityana travelled to the Western Cape while Biko went to Natal and the Transvaal. 'We actually never sat down to agree about what we would say,' Pityana reflected, 'but it was, more or less, that it's about time that black people up and down the country began to speak together in one voice.' 'Black' meant all of the oppressed, which included anyone classified 'Coloured', 'Indian' or 'Asian' as well as those classified 'Bantu'. This new definition had a liberating effect on many people, freeing them from the categories defined by apartheid, though some were extremely dubious of something that sounded as though it smacked of racism. It took time to sow the seed. Biko and Pityana were in constant contact, travelling and writing each other long letters to keep in touch: 'He was a political writer and was very good at throwing out ideas,' Pityana emphasised. Biko displayed another quality too, 'an eye to discern people and human nature in a very penetrating way without having to get into great discussions about things'. Biko and Pityana spent most of the early months of 1969 doing the rounds of the university campuses across the country.

The result of all this energy, enthusiasm and growing conviction amongst the black student youth was the founding of the South African Students' Organisation (Saso) in July 1969 at one of the government's own tribalised universities, Turfloop (the University of the North). Biko was its first president. The first SASO communiqué has a breathless quality about it:

1. At a time when events are moving so fast in the country, it is not advisable to show any form of division amongst students' ranks – especially now that students appear to be a power to be reckoned with in this country.
2. Any move that tends to divide the student population into separate laagers on the basis of colour is in a way tacit submission to having been defeated and apparently seems in agreement with apartheid.
3. In a racially sensitive country like ours, provisions for racially exclusive bodies tend

Barney Pityana (centre), who was elected president of Saso to succeed Biko in July 1970.

Father Aelred Stubbs.

Neville Curtis.

37

to build up resentment and to widen the gap that exists between the races, and the student community should resist all attempts to fall into this temptation.

4. Any formation of a purely non-white body shall be subject to a lot of scrutiny and so the chances of the organisations lasting are very little.

Coincidentally, at this time, Nusas itself underwent some radical changes under the presidency of Neville Curtis, an independent-thinking 'outsider' who was not definable in the Nusas liberal tradition. Curtis and Biko met at conferences on several occasions. They both wanted to find a way of working on black and white campuses alike that was fresh and innovative and not just defensive; that would, said Curtis, 'enable us to mobilise students, that allowed us to *raise* issues, not just react to issues'. Though their tasks were different, the two had a breadth of vision that acknowledged the usefulness, at that point, of the continued existence of both organisations, co-operating but not coming under one umbrella.

Saso could have wrecked Nusas, but instead it passed a resolution recognising the latter as the national student body. By keeping this contact with Curtis, Biko picked up some of Nusas's most useful

Steve Biko addresses a meeting of SASO's second General Students Council held at the University of Natal, July 1971.

procedures, particularly the idea of training, which in Saso became known as formation schools. They concentrated on leadership training, which at the same time ensured that layers of leadership would persist. This was not only as a precaution in case people were 'knocked off' by the government but as a principle to avoid hierarchy. Both organisations were in a situation where neither might survive. Nusas and the UCM

39

had the universities and the Church to draw on; Saso had neither. 'It was an extremely brave venture in organisational terms,' Neville Curtis recalls.

Biko built up different groups of people with whom he debated and discussed ideas and procedures. In February 1970 he wrote a letter to the presidents of all the SRCs of the English- and Afrikaans-speaking universities, to national student organisations and students overseas, giving the historical background, the structure, policy and aims of Saso.

In this letter the word 'non-white' was still used, but this was to be short-lived. 'Non-white' was a negation of being. It indicated a desire to become white eventually. It implied that 'whiteness' was the norm to which one attached all other people whose own culture and identity had been negated. It was soon removed from Saso's vocabulary. Mpumlwana elaborates: 'Over time, blacks had been made to see themselves as just a mass, one of a mass without any sense of responsibility about who you are, your destiny and your society. Just "non-whites", non-something. Everything that you are has been taken away from you. You're a non-person. In order to be a person you have got to claim your identity. You name yourself. And we named ourselves "black".'

In July 1970 Pityana became second president of Saso, and Biko editor of the *SASO Newsletter*. From

August Biko began his column 'I Write What I Like' and signed it 'Frank Talk'. Throughout the following two years it enabled the evolution of the philosophy of Black Consciousness to be recorded and expressed, ideas sounded out with colleagues and friends, tried and tested in the Saso style of consensus politics.

In January 1971 Pityana and Biko delivered two separate papers to an Abe Bailey conference in Cape Town, statements that were 'a major refinement of what we were doing'. Barney recalls how incredible it was that neither of them had read each other's paper in advance. As they had dealt with the far more ideological question of whether or not they should participate, it was quite clear to both of them, in the papers presented, 'that there was a lot there between us that was actually a result of conversations and writing and sharing and thinking through precisely how you present, in a hostile, in an ambiguous and uncertain climate, something positive and, in our view, certain. We felt certain about the capacity of black people to participate in their own struggle but that it needed to be said in a challenging and in a critical way.'

A particular style of leadership evolved which recognised the enormous advantage of widespread consultation. This meant not only consultation to win over a proposal but the creation of an atmosphere where individual opinions were considered and taken seriously. They were valued equally. It was time-consuming and costly in energy but it ensured true development and growth, both politically and in terms of human advance, so that people became more efficient and confident. This style was effective for Black Consciousness and developed at the height of some of the most oppressive years of apartheid. Its legacy and the whole leadership-training style remain relevant today in a country still grappling with crime and the effects of migrant labour, which destroyed family life; with one of the widest gaps between rich and poor in the world; where the burden of a previous inferior education system persists; where self-worth has been ravaged by the onslaught of HIV/Aids, coincidental with growing violence against women and children.

Black Consciousness drew intellectual and political inspiration and dialogue from the Civil Rights and Black Power movements in the United States, from Négritude and other forms of post-colonial thinking and writing in Africa. It concerned itself with the religious movements of Ethiopianism and African religious political prophecy, and some of its practices were confirmed and strengthened through the methods of Paulo Freire's rapidly spreading pedagogy. All this was fervently debated in a growing consciousness rooted in the South African situation. The impact was that, under the very gaze of a severely oppressive

Biko with fellow medical students Brigette Savage, Rogers Ragavan and Ben Ngubane.

regime, people began to live lives actively aware of forging their own identity. A fearlessness evolved. The aim of Black Consciousness was that this style of life should filter into the lives of all the oppressed, the vast majority of South Africans. It sought to use the greatest potential of each person, *any* person, within its ranks, never considering anyone incapable of contributing. Initiated in Saso, this was to become the hallmark of the Black Consciousness Movement as a whole. Because it was a lived experience, recognition of a new identity became an integral part of its proponents. In so far as was possible, leadership was rendered invisible. This was not only in preparation for the inevitable moment when the State would single people out to be banned, banished or arrested, but also an acknowledgement that multiple skills are the most productive.

Biko's personality had a large part to play in living and nurturing this style. His presence ensured that people would be heard and their opinion considered. He engendered trust and freed people to use their potential. To him it was clear that to obtain the common goal of a true humanity, the game of power politics would have no place – a spectre that haunts the ruling ANC today. He recognised and enabled participation in such a way that the sum of the whole was richer, more useful and politically more powerful when thoroughly worked through than that of individual leadership and domination. Time was needed for a group to identify the skills in one another and then to trust those skills so that delegation could take place with the urgency and speed that were often necessary. Pityana describes Biko as 'the person who brought ideas. He was the fundamentalist, if you like, the person who brought the basic ideas which were being bandied about and thrown around. He was actually quite stubborn in some ways because he was very keen to push his point and his ideas to the limit.' For this reason the very opposite of consensus politics might have been expected from a person like Biko. This was not so. He himself was also challenged by equally vocal and questioning people, which he encouraged. And although he talked a lot, he also listened. He did not dominate and he had the capacity to be delighted by counter-argument.

Biko's room in the old army barracks of the medical student residence, Alan Taylor, doubled up as the Saso office. Saso became a sub-culture of the university. It was there, Mpumlwana recalls, when he first came to UNNE, that you 'expected to find people in some conversation or another; very friendly people, warm and accommodating, non-hierarchical and always involved in debates, conversations, always something exciting with a new angle to develop'.

Everybody read books outside their university subjects. These provided the essence of the debates and the discussion that made the future have some kind of meaningful possibility. Many people were involved, people who later became psychologists, doctors, poets, writers, politicians and trade unionists. Among them were Charles Sibisi, who was considered the 'international' expert, while Mamphela Ramphele and Malusi Mpumlwana worked on practical community programmes; Mandla Langa had started writing poetry and was getting it published in journals by small publishing houses in Johannesburg; Strini and Sam Moodley, Asha Rambally and Saths Cooper were founding members of the Theatre Council of Natal (Tecon), a group that was concerned with creating 'relevant theatre' by producing plays and poetry readings to accompany student conferences.

To write and to perform became an intrinsic part of the many meetings, teach-ins and seminars held throughout the country, and the General Student Councils (GSCs). Mandla Langa recalls: 'You would find yourself with a certain captive audience, people who would criticise you or encourage you but who would be there to read your stuff and try and make sense out of it. Students were extremely instrumental in making sure that one continued writing.' This included writers like Mafika Gwala, Mongane Wally Serote, Njabulo Ndebele, Strini Moodley and Saths Cooper, who, working alongside musicians and performing theatre groups, all interpreted with anger, depth and humour 'the thrust of that time'. The very nature of being 'travelling players', Serote remembers, gave them a consciousness and a 'global understanding' of the problems in the country.

In political and theological matters Biko and Pityana led the field. Langa recalls how 'we started sharing libraries, sharing books and also going to all these bookshops which had all these expensive books which we needed and, you know, finding a way of appropriating them. We started widening our vistas and our minds by reading books which the regime never possibly thought we'd lay our hands on, anything from the [Heinemann] African Writers Series to, well, we read Marcuse, we read the existential philosophers such as Jean-Paul Sartre. There was Mphahlele and maybe some hidden copies by Alex La Guma, Lewis Nkosi, Can Themba, Nat Nakasa, Bloke Modisane. We read all that.'

One of the most significant writers whom Biko passed on to the others was Frantz Fanon. It seemed coincidental that Fanon's work was published in English for the first time in 1965. Born in Martinique, Fanon had studied medicine in France and practised psychiatry in the Antilles, where he wrote *Black Skin, White Masks,* a psychological and philosophical analysis of the state of being black, and then *The Wretched of the Earth,* a book which included theory on the colonising of the mind, experience of which he gained when working in Algeria during the French-Algerian colonial war. Another important writer was James Cone, the black American theologian. Malcolm X was the 'Black Consciousness' counterpart to the liberal integrationism of Martin Luther King. He published his autobiography in 1965 and the Saso group had twelve gramophone records of his speeches. 'Compared to Martin Luther King, we felt that Malcolm's preachings were much more gutsy, much more in tandem with what we were thinking and feeling. They were also very very influential in some of the plays which we wrote and performed.' Mandla Langa recalls that there was also a resonance with the kind of cultural awakening expressed by the Black Panthers, and 'consciously or unconsciously there was a lot of borrowing, which is why you find the poetry of that time became very derivative really'.

One of the main sources for information about relevant books came from the 'objectionable books' listed in the South African *Government Gazette* itself. Quite obviously these were the very books that became required reading. Pityana also recalls how a man in the United States consulate made much of the relevant American literature available while another source was a Lutheran bookshop which unobtrusively sold banned books.

Thorough discussion took place as a constant backdrop to student activity. In preparation for the 1971 GSC, regarding leadership training, Biko (now 25) began to make an extensive study of South African political movements, concentrating on the early so-called religious breakaways of the 1890s, the Ethiopian movement, the foundation of the ANC, the history of the Industrial and Commercial Workers' Union (ICU), and so forth. *Time Longer than Rope* was a favourite book. Pityana recalls much of this research as a 'subconscious act of transcending the visions of the past without denying the authenticity of that'. At the same time there was a clear recognition that 'we could no longer proceed on that same basis [to] capture the imagination of our people'.

And so a new energy and mood began to spread across the country. Without making him stand out too much, nobody would question that much of the setting in motion of that rolling spirit was initiated by Biko, or affirmed by Biko. Once moving, once in motion, he stepped back and others took over, and they, in turn, did the same. He was always of the belief that nobody should become cast in a mould, that diversity was educative, that people had different skills. No Saso president, for example, was in office for more than a year, a precedent set by Biko. This capacity to stand back, to put others forward, to initiate new ideas, get something going and make it practical, meant that although Biko was present, he managed not to be dominant. It was an infusion of ideas which he encouraged, resulting in a newly found energy that began to perpetuate itself country-wide.

He travelled extensively with different people. Not having a driving licence at this stage he always let others drive. 'It didn't matter where we were in South Africa, whether in rural areas, in townships, in town, in the suburbs, we always knew where to go, which shebeen to go to. We would arrive in a place, sometimes at three in the morning, when usually everything is shut. We would knock, the person would say "no", but as soon as they heard it was us they would open and we would get six boxes of beer, two quarts of whiskey and a *gumba* (dance party) started,' Serote recalls. 'We would all be tired and I would fall asleep and I would wake up and Steve would still be on his chair, talking and drinking. And the thing that struck you was his great joy at being among people. This seemed to inspire him, this seemed to give him the energy and even the willingness to challenge, you know. I think the *gumba* situation at that time was a very very important forum for us. Under a relaxed atmosphere we were able, then, to explore a whole lot of very complex issues, informally, of course always with Steve presiding.'

In Johannesburg, as elsewhere, socialising took on a new form with the arrival of Saso. Since the 1950s, there had been a considerable 'crossing of the colour bar', as it was called, which mostly took place in white liberal and Communist homes. Bokwe Mafuna, then working for the *Rand Daily Mail*, remembers the ambivalence he and others often felt in performing the role of 'interpreters' of the black townships and the black world at these parties. He remembers being introduced to Biko by Stanley Sabelo Ntwasa, the UCM's roving representative, at a 'garden party'. When Saso began to be active around that time, a new forum was established. Mafuna says that 'they were neither the quiet, intellectual discourse, sitting and drinking in the white suburbs nor were they getting drunk in

Mamphela Ramphele addresses the first Black People's Convention, December 1972.

the shebeen. They were social events which had a lot of political significance, where people met one another from all over the country, where you could speak out, pour out your souls to one another', a place where things raised in that informal atmosphere would be transformed into resolutions for later conferences.

Mafuna recalls how he had never been in such an environment before. He had been a worker since school-going age and a member of trade unions before he became a photographer and journalist. 'I had grown up in an environment of conflict all my life and here, for once, I was with people with whom I could be at ease, among whom I could start believing in myself

51

… I found myself organising trade unions throughout the country. We went to Port Elizabeth, Cape Town, Durban, Johannesburg, all over. We were organising youth. We were organising women. All these things I had never believed I could do and we were getting other people to do them with us.' He later joined Saso's Black Workers' Project and spent many intimate moments with Biko travelling all over the country, with the resultant hours of long discussions which ensue on long journeys across the vast landscape. 'Steve respected people and he made people respect each other. His whole attitude and his whole experience was a working-class attitude and experience. He had extraordinary gifts of knowing how to relate to people and be able to inspire confidence in people, and trust.'

Biko's style of leadership was similar when tensions arose in student or political meetings. With his various caucuses he usually worked through his ideas in advance. He stuck to them but also had the flexibility of recognising and accepting a majority voice. What is more, it is clear that he was concerned to look at the long-term, wider picture, and not get caught up in the emotional frustration of the moment. He had the capacity to allow things to happen without needing or trying to 'control' them, but would assume leadership when he saw possibilities of division or short-term misunderstanding. Father Stubbs speaks of Biko as having 'this deep-rooted profound intuition of togetherness. He wanted to be in the background. He couldn't be in the background in any ultimate sort of way. He wanted other people to take the lead. I think it was his intuition of what real leadership involves.'

4

To love and to work

'Freud was once asked what he thought a normal person should be able to do well,' Erik Erikson tells us. And Freud had replied: 'Lieben und arbeiten', to love and to work. Erikson goes on to say that 'it pays to ponder on this simple formula; it grows deeper as you think about it. For when Freud said "love", he meant the generosity of intimacy as well as genital love; when he said "love and work", he meant a general work productiveness which would not preoccupy the individual to the extent that he might lose his right or capacity to be a sexual and loving being.'

Work
Biko's work was to awaken the people: first, from their own psychological oppression through recognising their inferiority complex and restoring their self-worth, dignity, pride and identity; secondly, from the mental and physical oppression of living in a white racist

society. Biko explained: 'I had a man working on one of our projects in the Eastern Cape on electricity … a white man with a black assistant. He had to be above the ceiling and the black man was under the ceiling and they were working together pushing up wires and pushing through the rods in which the wires are and so on, and all the time there was insult, insult, insult from the white man. "Push this, you fool." That sort of talk. And of course this touched me. I knew the white man very well, he spoke well to me, so we invited them to tea and I asked him: "Why do you speak like this to this man?" And he said to me in front of the guy: "This is the only language he understands, he is a lazy bugger." And the black man smiled. I asked him if it was true and he said: "I am used to him." This sickened me. I thought for a moment that I did not understand black society. After some two hours I came back to this black guy and said to him: "Did you really mean it?" The man changed. He became very bitter. He was telling me how he wanted to leave his job, but what could he do? He did not have any skills, he had no assurances of another job, his job was to him some form of security, he had no reserves. If he did not work today he could not live tomorrow, he had to work, he had to take it. And as he had to take it he dared not show any form of insolence to his boss.'

What mattered to Biko, Mpumlwana explained,

was what work *he* needed to do in order for this person to be himself all the time. He further understood that self-realisation and identity also depended on seizing the necessary tools to function in a technological world, tools deliberately denied blacks by the Bantu Education Act. As Dr Verwoerd, Minister of Native Affairs at the time, had explained in parliament, when speaking about the new laws of segregated education: 'There is no place for [the Bantu] in the European [white] community above the level of certain forms of labour … For that reason it is of no avail for him to receive a training which has as its aim absorption in the European community above the level of certain forms of labour … Up till now he has been subjected to a school system which drew him away from his own community and partially misled him by showing him the green pastures of the European but still did not allow him to graze there.'

Demanding those denied tools – at the same time recognising that the green pastures of white education were not so green after all – would lead to widespread disruption in the Bantu Education system, which was sustained by black students for a whole generation over the next two decades. In 1972, although reluctant to believe he could not manage both studying and political work, Biko chose the more difficult political road. This was formally affirmed by his dismissal from medical school in June 1972, having only officially passed three years out of six. What was more painful was that he would also have to disappoint his family's ambitions for him and those of virtually the whole Ginsberg community. The choice he made was one that thousands of black students would come to face: the choice of either becoming a political activist or taking the time to gain some sort of qualification towards a professional life, with inevitable compromises, under apartheid. Biko thus sacrificed his chance of becoming a professional doctor. For the time being, his work lay elsewhere.

Two months later, in August 1972, he joined Bennie A. Khoapa as a staff member of the Black Community Programmes (BCP), whose offices, at 86 Beatrice Street, Durban, were on the same premises as Saso. This programme was concerned to develop skills in the black community. 'Issues of empowerment, the development of the ability to decide, the ability to be critical', were some of these – as well as to create practical programmes to meet sheer need, Khoapa explained. Biko's brief was primarily to co-ordinate youth leadership training and thereby 'expand the thrust of conscientising to youth beyond the schools'. He worked closely with Harry Ranwedzi Nengwekhulu. Youth groups already existed, country-wide, and many of them were well defined. They consisted not only of

'At the heart of this kind of thinking is the realisation by blacks that the most potent weapon in the hands of the oppressor is the mind of the oppressed.' – Biko's address on 'White Racism and Black Consciousness', Cape Town, January 1971.

pupils in school but also those who had had to drop out of school early, for economic reasons, most of them now on the streets but also some young workers in industry.

In this regard Biko recognised the importance of the educational methodology of Paulo Freire. He had read his book *Pedagogy of the Oppressed,* and in July had sought out Anne Hope, who was running training courses on Freire's educational method in Johannesburg and Swaziland. Fifteen people enrolled, including Pityana, Mafuna, Cooper, Moodley, Johnny Issel, Mthuli Shezi, Jerry Modisane, Deborah Matshoba and others. They attended workshops over four months. Each month's session consisted of five days of intensive training, after which they returned to their local communities for three weeks of research and practice. Key to Freire's methodology is the recognition that teaching should be a political act, directly related to production, health, social conditions, to the regular system of instruction, and to the overall plan for a society still to be realised in the future. The act of teaching should not be separated from the act of learning. The trainees, therefore, needed to be able to submerge themselves in the context of the learners' life experience, primarily to be able to listen while encouraging learners to unveil and 'unpackage' their lives and problems. Listening did not mean only literally hearing but listening in order to create a curriculum or a meaningful training programme for people out of what they disclosed about themselves. This training influenced Biko considerably and dovetailed with his style of leadership.

In the meantime BCP had applied to the Ford Foundation for funds to produce a state-of-the-black-nation annual review, similar to the annual survey of the Institute of Race Relations but written, researched and produced by blacks. Ford favoured Race Relations. Undeterred, Biko set about organising the first issue of the *Black Review*. Khoapa says this was virtually paid for out of the petty cash of the Black Community Programmes and, as Biko explained, could be realised with 'the help of some boys who are being chucked out of school and are not going back to university, like Welile Nhlapo and Tomeka Mafole'. Biko assured Khoapa that 'All they need is some food and transport. I am sure they'll be glad to do the paper, the coordination and so on'. Biko was the editor. However, by the time it was printed in 1973 Biko had been banned. This banning order prevented him from preparing any material for publication, and so *Black Review* came out under Khoapa's name and was dedicated to Biko and Mafuna, who was also banned.

Early in that new year Biko enrolled for a law degree through the correspondence university, Unisa

– the degree his father had also aspired to. In this and in his decision to continue with his political work, he selected the career from which his relatives had sought to protect him and pursued his vision. Legal training would add professional skills to his natural intelligence and curiosity and add weight to his ability to take hold of facts and thrash them out. He already had the African gift of *ubuntu*, being a person for other people.

Generosity of intimacy

'He was best at helping you be who *you* are best,' Mpumlwana explains. Indeed, most people who knew Biko well felt an intimacy of their very own with him. He gave them his undivided attention, entrusted them to recognise their own potential, whether it was a friend, fellow student, lover, spiritual father, teacher or someone in authority. This intimacy did not often engender rivalry. It was part of his capacity to love generously, and he spent a great deal of his time giving each person his undivided attention.

Neville Curtis, Nusas president, recalls him in those student days as 'an incredibly attractive human being. He was good-looking and articulate. He was a sparkler, a vivid person, a wonderful person. He could hardly ever talk to you without putting his arm around you. And also this "no bullshit" thing.' At the same time 'he was far from a perfect personality, a perfect human being. He was apt to over-indulge, but he was living life to the full and doing it with vividness and style.'

This generosity of intimacy naturally grew in complexity when it involved women, a complexity he largely chose to ignore. In those early travelling days there was an element of exploitation towards women which certainly bordered on chauvinism. With his 'vividness and style', Biko gained the reputation of being a 'womaniser'. His view of himself was that he was always open. People could take it or leave it. There was a certain defiance in his attitude, reminiscent of his defiance against authority. Sexism, as being potentially similar in form to racism, did not enter his head. Even when it was pointed out to him by women in the groups he worked in, he tended to set it aside. Like those in the ANC and in other liberation movements in Africa, he possibly held the view that Black Consciousness would liberate everything at once. Dimza Pityana affirms that the women who were involved in the Black Consciousness Movement were involved as blacks, not as black *women*. However, 'there was an interesting disjuncture between the genuine comradeship one experienced within the movement and the sexism which reared its head at many levels,' Mamphela Ramphele recalls. 'For example, the responsibility for catering, cleaning-up and other entertainment functions tended to fall on women participants.' And 'becoming one of the boys' contained simultaneous approval and disapproval. 'Late nights, alcohol consumption and smoking became part of life' but 'the same men one socialised with took a dim view of women being seen doing the same things as them publicly, especially smoking.' At the same time, feminism, which had swept through Europe and the US, was seen as 'irrelevant to the needs of black women in South Africa' and dismissed 'as a "bra-burning" indulgence of bored, rich white Americans'. And thus 'interpersonal relationships remained largely unchanged, with the man as the dominant partner, and many women remaining trapped in unsatisfactory relationships that violated their dignity as people'.

Basically, Biko was insatiably curious. He loved people. He found exploring relationships consistently fascinating, and though his exploration bordered on exploitation and might lead to complications which he sometimes did not know how to handle, he was someone seldom without love and respect. Being the person he was, he was much sought after by women and did not hesitate to have relationships with many of them. Pityana, on looking back, feels that Biko had not yet come 'to judge for himself how much you could have a fulfilled relationship with a woman without all the sexual overtones'. At the same time, he observed, in the circles that emerged, it was also true that 'many of the women [themselves] did not accept that there could be an authentic relationship with a man without that relationship becoming sexually loaded'. Serote observed that 'When you looked at the women around Steve, whom you knew he had personal relationships with, somehow the relationship between them had made something bloom – put lots of energy into every one of them. Even in relations like that he would continuously discuss these very complex issues, so many of the women had no choice but to continuously be conscientised and politicised!'

Women are often drawn to men who manifest the winning combination of power and human understanding – Martin Luther King, John F. Kennedy and Nelson Mandela immediately spring to mind. Biko was still a young man and was not in that kind of political limelight. Nevertheless, he had a similar ease of manner and charisma that was magnetic. Pityana maintains that one of the reasons that so many people wanted to be associated with him was this very capacity to 'radiate joy and confidence, which gave people a sense of ease and of love'. He accepted people, all people, without prejudice. Even the Security Police he knew must be human and, initially, he appealed to that. If that potential humanity continued to hide itself he virtually demanded it by his action and behaviour. It was only when he finally gave up on somebody that he sometimes became very angry. He accepted people first and then challenged them and, in risking his own generosity of intimacy, this usually had a profound effect on them. There was certainly no apparent seeking of power. Father Stubbs had the sense that Biko was somewhat wary of this potential power within him and that his saving grace was his recognition of his own vulnerability. This enabled him to be open.

This kind of challenge, these relationships, not only enriched him personally but were the way he chose to become informed about his country. The parties and shebeening, apart from being an important antidote to his intense lifestyle, also provided the forum, the access to a variety of people he might otherwise never have met. Sometimes he did not assess correctly the emotional impact of his behaviour on others, and there were certainly times when he got himself into relationships he had not bargained for. Although he read and digested many materials and books immediate to his task, it was people who became the library of his life.

Love and marriage
Freud, by his own definition, would have found Steve Biko 'normal'. His love seemed bound to set people free and he certainly knew how to work. Work was seldom without a circle or group of others, without consultation

Steve Biko with his wife, Ntsiki, and his son Nkosinathi.

with colleagues and the trust of friends. Later he exhibited a fearlessness and a powerful reasonableness that demanded respect even from the Security Police. Biko never lost 'his capacity to be a sexual and loving being'. Indeed, as we have seen, this capacity led to some complexity in his relationships. Few of these, however, had significant bearing on the two basic relationships which were of paramount importance to him. These attachments were different and deeply personal. They ran parallel, each one fulfilling different dimensions and needs in his life, and he never found it possible to give up one for the other. One was with Ntsiki Mashalaba, who became his wife, and the other, Mamphela Ramphele, his colleague at medical school, who grew visibly in his presence and who became the doctor of the first BCP clinic, Zanempilo, near King William's Town, where she put into action much of the theory of Black Consciousness.

By 1969 Ramphele had known Biko casually for about a year, and had met him regularly in the Saso circle as she became part of it. She remembers a sense of deep attraction for him then, which she dutifully ignored as she was engaged to be married to 'home-boy' Dick Mmabane at the end of the year. In early 1970 she returned to medical school, married, and excitedly displaying wedding photographs and rings. It was only later that she discovered that Biko had written her a letter, which she never received, encouraging her to delay her marriage. Ramphele was 22. Biko met Nontsikelelo (Ntsiki) Mashalaba and they were married at the end of 1970. They were both 23.

Ntsiki was training as a midwife at King Edward VIII Hospital in Durban. On their marrying, Biko's mother gave her the name Nosizwe – meaning 'Mother of the Nation' – warning her that 'your husband's name is Bantu and you are Nosizwe and you must know you are going to have lots of people around you'. Later Steve and Barney Pityana found a four-roomed house in Durban and Nosidima (Dimza) Pityana, Barney's wife, joined them. The relationship between the two women was warm and easy as they became good friends. During those few years they played a more or less accepted traditional role, sharing their first two babies, Nkosinathi (Biko) and Loyiso (Pityana), who were virtually the same age. They also had the nursing profession in common, Ntsiki having finished her midwifery by the time she got married, Dimza still completing hers.

Nontsikelelo Biko, small and dark with large soft eyes, describes herself then as quiet. 'I was very quiet indeed,' she explained, particularly when she went to medical school and listened to the discussions, seldom participating but absorbing a great deal. She was a private person, owning herself but creating a sense of ease and welcome around her. 'You feel very safe with Ntsiki,' Dimza explains, 'and very comfortable. She was a non-threatening person.' 'Still waters,' says Malusi Mpumlwana.

Their house was always full of people, who would arrive with or without Biko, at any time of the day or night. The main room more often than not contained sleeping bodies in the mornings: people from Saso, students from different universities throughout the country, and others. 'The money was short, short! But because we were working together with Barney, at least we managed to have good meals,' Ntsiki recalls. 'Sometimes we cooked meat, meat which would have been enough for the whole month!' Biko expected everybody to be fed, as they had been in his mother's house, even when they were very poor. Although Biko led such a politically demanding life, Ntsiki chose not to get involved in that side in a superficial way, but to play a supportive role to this life. Biko, on his side, believed in his commitment to his family, loved Ntsiki, and, whenever he was there, nurtured his children. They loved being with him, this huge father, strong and full of humour. Later, in King William's Town, he sometimes took Samora (his younger son) to the office, forgetting to bring clean nappies to change him, to the infuriation of his co-worker and secretary Nohle Mohapi. 'He was often away from home but I accepted him as he was,' says Ntsiki, 'a husband deeply involved in his politics. I very much accepted him.' He used to say when he brought his friends over: 'This is my wife, she's the people's wife, but we mustn't share her!'

And yet he expected her to share him. This type of expectation, this particular attitude towards his wife, highlights the ambiguity that existed within Biko. While he questioned just about everything else, he accepted, without question, a traditional view of the role of a wife, and this included her total loyalty under all circumstances. His mother, to whom he was dedicated all his life, was herself a powerful model, a woman whose home and personality had enabled the community of Ginsberg to be welcomed, to be accepted in the true sense of community. And Ntsiki complied, as young wives willingly do, not knowing what great demands would be made on her in her marriage to Steve Biko, demands which, ironically, set her questioning and led her later to claim her own self-image with dignity and independence. Biko's expectations required what amounted to an inordinate degree of tolerance and forbearing. Deep down he wished and hoped to make a real go with his family and children, but he soon realised, Pityana explained, that, as with his medical studies, this would not be possible. As his political commitment grew, things which he had expected to stay in place were submerged in its wake.

Biko was often obliged to work late at night and would sometimes remain in medical residence, where the Saso office still flourished. Amongst many others, he found himself working regularly alongside Mamphela Ramphele. She remembers how, in 1971, she got more and more involved with his thinking in the writing of the 'Frank Talk' articles. A dynamic, exciting, symbiotic relationship grew up between them, their skills complementing one another in many ways. A new energy was born. Being alongside Biko, Ramphele admits that she learnt a great deal about how to relate to people. On the other hand, Ramphele's capacity to transform ideas into practical action made her presence strengthening and critically relevant to him. Apart from her obvious intelligence, she was disciplined and totally reliable. They were two powerfully attractive people and their attraction for one another rapidly grew in depth, both politically and personally.

Soon after Steve married Ntsiki, Ramphele separated from her husband. She was very upset but, once back at medical school and into the swing of things, she increasingly became her own person, her inhibitions disappeared and, as her colleague Jay Pillay says, she 'became very very energetic'. She removed her wig, and was more and more conscious of being proud of being black, sometimes expressing it with anger and verve.

Biko became bound into two relationships. In most cases, under these circumstances, choices and sacrifices eventually have to be made. But, until he died at the age of 30, Biko did not make them. All three people lived with another's shadow cast over them, sometimes more encompassing than at other times. Changing circumstances constantly affected their lives and equilibrium, but the complexity of this triangle remained. Both Ntsiki and Mamphela bore two of Steve's children. Ntsiki had two boys: Nkosinathi (1971) and Samora Mzontsundu (1975). Mamphela had a girl, Lerato (1974), who died at two months, and a boy, Hlumelo (1978), born after Biko's death.

It would be too bald to leave it at that. Biko was deeply sensitive and agonised over many things. This situation often moved into sharp focus, demanding some resolution, especially when his relationship with Mamphela became more open and public, moving beyond a student affection into a powerful force. It was difficult to contain it without exposing its dynamic, and a vow they made early on, when it had begun to grow, not to hurt Ntsiki, was not sustained. She was deeply hurt by this relationship.

It is difficult to know whether (and, if so, when) Biko felt a real need to face these circumstances. The fact that he never *acted* to change them indicates that for a long while either he did not know how to or they were more acceptable to him as they were, unchanged. Father Stubbs raised the matter with him in 1974 just as he was leaving the Zanempilo clinic after a visit. Whether it was a shock coming from his 'dear priest' or whether he felt it to be a slight on his judgment, Biko was hurt and reacted with uncharacteristic anger. 'I regard topics of this nature as being extremely private. I am in many instances aware of the complexity that can be introduced by a willingness to accommodate the feelings of friends in a matter that is essentially private between two – or in this case three – parties. I have never found it necessary to reflect on my friends' private activities except in so far as I thought they affected at any one stage their political standing and their performance. Similarly I could never wish to ask you about your love life, your sexual life, etc. because I regard that as strictly speaking your business.'

He went on to make a more general observation: 'There is a profound difference in the way Westerners basically believe in character analysis to that adopted by us here. In many discussions I used to have with David [Russell] I agreed with him in comparing our attitude on the whole to that of the European working-class approach to life. When you guys talk about a person you tear him apart, analyse the way he speaks, looks at someone, thinks; you find a motive for everything he does; you categorise him politically, socially, etc. In

Steve Biko and Mamphela Ramphele outside the East London Magistrate's Court during one of Biko's many appearances for breaking his banning order.

short you are not satisfied until you have really torn him apart and have really parcelled off each and every aspect of his general behaviour and labelled it.' He admits, in the same letter, however, that in the political sphere he had learnt to do these things himself. Did he feel, then, that it was all right, and maybe useful, to subject politics to what he describes as a Western analysis, but that his personal decisions were fiercely and culturally his own, in spite of affecting friends and colleagues around him? In Xhosa culture the cautioning of a young man by an older man would be acceptable; moreover, Steve had been brought up as a Christian. The puzzle was too great and too sensitive for rational answers. In someone who seldom failed to look at problems head on and act on them in order to solve them, Biko in this instance was defiant, not yet ready for the solution. He obviously decided to live with these circumstances the way they were, in some ways refusing to see the implications in his usual clear, rational and human way. And then, there was the daily reality and, thereby, the rationale, of never giving it sufficient time. It was only in prison, in 1976, during a forced 101 days of solitary confinement, that he indicated he had begun to ponder this side of his life more fully and seriously.

5

Bantu – Son of Man, 1973–1977

In October 1972, aged 25, Biko was interviewed by Gail Gerhart, the American academic and writer. In discussing the apartheid government Biko said that if they were intelligent, they could 'create a capitalist black society'; that South Africa was one country in Africa where blacks might compete favourably with whites in industry, commerce and other professions. If they created this, 'South Africa could succeed [in putting across] to the world a pretty convincing, integrated picture with still 70 per cent of the population being underdogs!' However, whites were terribly afraid of this and, instead, were creating 'the best economic system for revolution'. The way they were going about it made communication among blacks easier, made the 'communication of ideas' possible through a shared, common stimulus as no physical or intellectual distance existed. 'In this whole conscientising programme, this is what makes ideas easily flow amongst people; this common ghetto experience blacks are subjected to.'

Banning

Black Consciousness was a philosophy which grew directly out of a racist State. It seized the very word 'black', defined by the State as the innately inferior majority, and transformed 'being black' into a defiance against that State. In his famous phrase, Biko detached any aspirations to 'white' values and said bluntly: 'Black man, you're on your own'.

By 1972 Biko predicted that it was obvious the government would become more vigilant and would take more definite action against the movement. 'But,' he went on to say, 'it's too late in a sense. We don't need an organisation to push the kind of ideology we are pushing. It's there. It's already been planted. It's in the people. We've got a very broad front, which is completely unintimidated. This constant change in leadership in Saso is partly to accommodate a very quick gradation of people to a certain level.' Although BCP contained few workers, it is interesting to note that in the first three months of 1973 the dockworkers, whose significant strikes in Durban changed history, refused to elect a leadership that could be identified.

When the first BC bannings came in March 1973, the movement was determined to treat them as a kind of hiccup. The State order immediately scattered eight of its leaders to different parts of the country, to whatever was their designated magisterial district:

Pityana to Port Elizabeth, Mafuna to Johannesburg, Biko to King William's Town, and so forth. They removed some of the current Saso office-bearers – Jerry Modisane, then president, and Harry Nengwekhulu, permanent organiser; they took out two of the founding members of the Theatre Council of Natal – Strini Moodley (also editor of the *SASO Newsletter*) and Saths Cooper (public relations officer for the Black People's Convention) – and Drake Koka, a founding member of BPC and general secretary of the Black Allied Workers' Union.

The address given in the banning order to Biko was that of his mother's house in Ginsberg. There he returned, empty-handed as it were, to the community that had funded an important part of his education. His mother remembers saying to him: 'Bantu, things are now hard for you. You are at home. You are doing nothing. When I was educating you I thought that by now I would be able to rest. Now, I am not resting. I cannot rest. You are imprisoned forever.'

Biko responded to her in the paradigm she best understood and asked her what Christ's mission on earth had been, and she replied, 'To save the oppressed.' Then he said: 'I too have a mission.' She remembers looking at him standing in the doorway of her house and realising that 'there was something deep in this child and I had an understanding of what was going on'.

Quite soon Mamcethe overcame her disappointment and became an ally, developing an expertise in dealing with the Security Police. Her open home now became home to all the young people who came to work in King William's Town. Although she never said so, she lived in fear of Biko's life night and day, and often lay awake until the early hours of the morning until she would hear his car return, the door open and she would know he was safe.

Very soon after his arrival Biko located the Anglican priest, David Russell, who had broken the news of his banning to his mother. Russell lived in a small house in the grounds of the church of St Chad's in the heart of King William's Town's white residential area: 15a Leopold Street. The church had not been used for a year because of the collapse of the roof and the subsequent move of the congregation to the local townships of Zwelitsha and Ginsberg. When Russell approached the priest-in-charge, James Gawe, they agreed it should be used as an office for Saso and BCP. Very shortly all three organisations were functioning there, the BCP existing through the facilities of the other two with no official status of its own, and a new committed community began to form.

Russell had his own agenda, which was well under way when Biko arrived. Speaking fluent Xhosa, he had taken up the cause of people removed, by legislation, from farms and towns like Middelburg and Burgersdorp, to an area in his parish called Dimbaza. This was one of many ill-prepared resettlement places in the homelands where blacks were forced to go, where there was no form of subsistence, no proper housing on arrival, where old people died of shock and infants of malnutrition. The state pensions were R5 a month, and for widows with children about R3 a month plus rations. Russell had first fasted on the steps of St George's Cathedral in Cape Town to draw attention to this, and then himself lived on R5 per month, for six months, writing a letter each month to the Minister responsible describing what meagre rations he could afford to buy.

Biko was undoubtedly drawn to Russell as a kindred spirit – not only intellectually but also finding him helpful and trusting him as a friend and confidant. Russell knew about local conditions, including the Security Police. Biko trusted Russell's political antennae and would enjoy dropping in on him at different times of the day or night to relax, letting slip his own political persona to discuss all kinds of issues – one of which was Russell's own stance and the nature of his commitment. When Russell explained that, as a priest, he was called to poverty, chastity and obedience, which included leading a celibate life, Biko was curious enough to test himself against these in the light of *his* own commitment and wrote a rare six-page document, which he and Russell discussed at length.

'Does God exist? I have never had problems with this question. I am sufficiently convinced of the inadequacy of man and the rest of creation to believe that a greater force than mortals is responsible for creation, maintenance and continuation of life. I am also sufficiently religious to believe that man's internal insecurity can only be alleviated by an almost enigmatic and supernatural force to which we ascribe all power, all wisdom and love ... God has laid for man certain basic laws that must govern interaction between man and man, man and nature at large. These laws I see as inscribed in the ultimate conscience of each living mortal.' He goes on to say that 'Obedience to God in the sense that I have accepted it is in fact at the heart of the conviction of most selfless revolutionaries. It is a call to men of conscience to offer themselves and sometimes their lives for the eradication of evil.'

Biko was a religious person in the broad sense of the word. Khoapa said Biko also knew that anybody who might try to influence the black population politically and de-emphasise religion would not succeed. In the document to Russell, Biko is at pains to be honest and grapple with the Christian faith, not only because he is talking to a Christian but also because he is exploring his own self in relation to the way he has absorbed some of that faith. Choosing the word 'revolutionary' distances him from the practice of the Church and seems to enable him the freedom to pursue obedience to conscience (what he calls 'ultimate conscience' as opposed to a person's own conscience) without the cloying aspects of an institution.

'To the revolutionary the Church is anti-progress and therefore anti God's wishes because long ago it decided not to obey God but to obey man; long ago the Church introduced segregated worship and segregated seminaries.' Further, the 'Churches have tended to complicate religion and theology' and 'to drive away the common man by immersing themselves in bureaucracy and institutionalisation'. Christ 'is so conservatively interpreted at times that I find him foreign to me. On the other hand if I accept him and ascribe to him the characteristics that flow logically from my contemplation about him and his work, then I must reject the Church almost completely.'

In Biko's definition, the Church as an institution was not so distant from other institutions like segregated schools and universities, which in turn were not distinct from the law and the State. In Biko's view all these were the antithesis of God's basic laws, and in working towards obedience to God as he saw it – the exploration towards his own 'ultimate conscience' – he fulfilled his definition of a selfless revolutionary by intuitively knowing before he died that he, too, would have to give his life for 'the eradication of evil'. 'I can reject all Churches and still be godly,' he wrote. 'I do not need to go to Church on Sunday in order to manifest "godliness".'

Early on, as we have seen, he had an intense dislike of mindless and destructive authority, and a healthy distaste for institutions that became ossified and limited and behaved accordingly. In the confined enclosure of apartheid he refused to be reactive to its system. Instead he ignored its desired psychological stranglehold and used its racism to forge a common cause with many others, a community dedicated to creative and practical action. He recognised that beneath the layered levels of anxiety and fear was a deep seam with which to work. He was convinced that the ground rules that made for human communication and interaction lay in coming to know this consciousness. This involved demanding in others an encounter with what was ultimately humane in them, a quality he sought and often brought forth. His life now turned him face-to-face with the law and the State in the form of both the Security Police and the courts. In this formidable encounter he was to put to the test his faith and the essence of who he was and what he understood, knowing that the revolutionary's task includes 'liberation not only of the oppressed but also of the oppressor'.

The culture of fearlessness

Banning was a drastic form of restriction. Essentially, banned people were put in charge of their own imprisonment. Movement was confined to a specific magisterial district – this was often the district where one was born – and could mean losing one's job if one worked elsewhere. It prevented one from entering any place of learning; from preparing anything for publication; from attending a gathering of any kind; from talking to the press. It prohibited a person from being with more than one other person at any time, even in his or her own home, and in some 'house-arrested' cases banned people had to report to the police once a week and were confined to their homes between the hours of 6 p.m. and 6 a.m., as if under a private curfew.

'Banning orders have a strong tendency to turn a person into a social leper', wrote David Russell, in the *Daily Dispatch* of 1 September 1973. 'The banned are legally innocent citizens incarcerated in an inhuman twilight existence. It is no exaggeration to say that banning is a form of violence; violence to justice, violence to family, violence to persons. [There is] no means of appeal or recourse to a just hearing. If he [Biko] has a meal with friends he can be dragged before the courts and smeared as a common criminal. He can be found guilty and sentenced to imprisonment for anything between one and ten years.'

As people were banned they were very closely watched by Security Police, who did everything to catch them out. Even if a person was meticulous, it was virtually impossible to live within the confines of the banning order. If one did, one began to despise oneself for being one's own jailer, which was exactly the psychological state of mind desired by the government, an unacceptable state for anyone involved in Black Consciousness. So life became a cat-and-mouse game.

The suppression came in waves. No sooner had the leadership of Saso, BPC and BCP, which was banned in March 1973, been replaced than those appointed were, in turn, banned in August; those who replaced the August people were banned in October, and so on. Harassment by the Security Police was relentless, and charges were constantly laid in a further attempt to secure impotence and a sense of despair.

How did the movement respond to the banning order? In King William's Town, to begin with, people were afraid of being seen with Biko. 'I mean, we had the police actually driving bumper to bumper behind us 24 hours a day, and that scared people,' Mpumlwana recalls. The basic principle was not to ban yourself but to let the police do all the work: to monitor the system, to have to trail around following people night and day, to be made to work hard to ensure that what they had implemented was their responsibility. 'So we didn't recognise the banning order in a sense. We put good locks on our doors. To all intents and purposes, if you're indoors the police have got no power.' There could be a party in one's house, but they would have to prove one was part of it. Mpumlwana laughed at the irony: 'You can't be held responsible for being in your house where the party is being held!' The banning order was studied, the loopholes found, and those banned began to interpret it for the police.

They also held to the principle of not being reckless, not giving the police the opportunity to have them in court. At the same time, Mpumlwana explained how 'we learnt not to trust lawyers' opinions on things. We found that they were very conservative legally, and so it was important, if you wanted to break the law, to make your own rules. If you happen to be wrong they will have to defend you, but don't ask them what is right!' This, in turn, led to a strategy of using the courts as a public forum. It was not new for South Africans, accused of political opposition, to use the dock for defence speeches, thus keeping alive historic political statements and realities which could be quoted down the years and put to use by the media and opposition world-wide, the most famous being the Rivonia Trial of 1963–4, at which Nelson Mandela made his memorable speech from the dock.

Black Consciousness, as such, was not banned, only individuals were. The courts could be used to their purpose as much as everything else, part of the defiance of every day. On the occasions when Biko, for example, was taken to court for infringement or violation of his banning order he displayed his new-found legal skills, having thought ahead before he broke the conditions as to what new legal point he could appeal to or what interpretation had not yet been tested. He was never jailed on that account. This helped strengthen the resistance of other banned people, who were isolated or particularly harassed by police vigilance, and of those in prison.

As banning persisted and detention without trial increased, the Black Consciousness style of leadership, passed on to many groups in formation schools and workshops, came into good effect. An indefinable community, country-wide, with no easily identifiable leadership was already in existence. And those banished by the State were never considered separate from the others. Rather, they were considered to have been 'relocated' and it was assumed they would become effective working in these areas. They were part of decision-making, part of a circuit, and were consulted. Just as in the early days Biko had visited the banned as a matter of course, this was extended to a wider community network created out of trust and regular interaction. Those people who could be, were constantly on the move. Pityana, who was banned in the tough Port Elizabeth district, remembers the extraordinary way in which each person, no matter where he or she was staying, would be considered. Nobody was allowed to feel abandoned, however remote and however harassed. Enormous risks were taken at times in order to ensure that this happened. Thenjiwe Mtintso, a Fort Hare student, who came to work in King William's Town, says that those around Biko often forgot he was restricted and admits that it was only later, when she herself was banned to Johannesburg, that she became aware of how Biko had 'given so much to us, politically and otherwise, done so much and lived under such pressure'. Biko was 26 when he was restricted.

It was necessary to become fearless, to conquer fear – the kind of quality that grows through exercise, explained Aelred Stubbs. 'They weren't polite, they were tough,' recalls David Russell, 'but they knew the kind of parameters of how tough you could be without overplaying your cards and so the [Security] Branch was scared of them. They didn't know how to handle them.' Russell recalls one incident when they raided Biko's home in Ginsberg at night. Biko asked them what they wanted. They usually said they had come to see if somebody was there or that they were looking for banned literature, or some such pretext. They wanted to go into rooms where people were asleep. Biko said, "Well, let me tell you now that you are not going into *that* room because that is where my mother sleeps and you're not going into *that* room," [indicating] where his brother-in-law was with his wife. But they *did* go in there. And he said: "You see what you are doing with yourselves; you are opening people's doors and looking at people sleeping in bed with their wives at night." Biko made them feel small. He was also angry and it was time they got out. He moved towards them, cigarette in one hand and put out the butt in the palm of his other hand. The police got a tremendous fright. He had, in fact, moved to flick it out of the window but they had thought he was going to attack them. He was big and physically strong. They were really thrown. They found it extremely difficult to handle his style, his intelligence, his statements; a man of that calibre. I think that set quite a tone of style for the grouping there.'

Biko challenged what was ultimately human in others. If those terms were not forthcoming he could be tough, as tough as anybody. Donald Woods reports one occasion when he was in an interrogation room, in detention, with 'seven security policemen standing along the walls all around him. [Warrant-Officer] Hattingh entered the room, walked straight up to where Steve was sitting, and slapped him hard across the face.

"'What happened then?" I [Woods] asked.

"'I hit him right against the wall," Steve replied. "Bust his false teeth."

"'Then what?"

"'He went straight out of the room. I had the feeling he didn't know what to do, or how to react, so he just went out – presumably for further instructions from his superiors.'"

This unhesitant response to insult was a direct display of how Biko exhibited fearlessness and how he practised Black Consciousness as a way of life. He was not going to be bullied. He considered banning as just one more of the innumerable restrictions that apartheid placed on black lives and refused to change his lifestyle in spite of the attempts by the State to watch him night and day. Although he seldom showed the strain, it may well have been the reason for his occasional, sudden and violent outbursts of anger at something of no great significance, when he would even hit out physically and it became very difficult to calm him.

Biko, like all of the others, consistently broke every single banning condition. In spite of being prohibited from preparing material for publication, he had completed the editing of *Black Review* and, later, was part of a team which prepared material for a regular newspaper column that the Black Consciousness point of view secured in the local East London paper, the *Daily Dispatch*. Biko often met more than one person at a time but was careful not to be seen to be doing so. He found a quiet place, within his magisterial district, near a dam, where he would drive with friends or visitors who came to consult him, to avoid the offices, which were bugged. If it was necessary he went out of his magisterial district. On many occasions he drove to see his wife, Ntsiki, when she worked in Keiskammahoek during the week; in 1974 he and Mpumlwana went to Durban after the arrest of most of the Saso–BPC leadership in 1974 to sort out problems there.

Banning failed to destroy the spirit and development of Black Consciousness. The next four years saw the flowering of some of the most imaginative and practical projects it was to produce. King William's Town became an important place where many people touched base, including international visitors. The arteries of contact persisted more fiercely, which included many of those banned. On one occasion at least, I myself witnessed, at a late-night *gumba*, Biko putting his finger over his lips each time he opened the door to admit one person after another, none of whom, according to the law, was permitted to be there. *Gumbas* remained a forum and an essential palliative against isolation.

Growth of a community

Biko asked Mpumlwana, who was then 22, to help him settle down and find people with whom to work, and the office in King William's Town was set up. Mpumlwana had already been alongside Biko in Durban. Late at night, after politicking or completing work on an issue or a Saso pamphlet, they would end the long hours with wrestling. 'It was our game. I enjoyed felling him. I'd played rugby. I'd go for his legs, lift him off and throw him down.' This was no mean feat as Mpumlwana was no match for Biko physically, being small and slightly built. Mpumlwana, a committed Christian, was unafraid of confrontation or of challenging values. With his wide-set, sensitive eyes alert to human suffering and humour alike, he was willing to pursue uncomfortable truths and often mediated crises involving warring political factions. Like Biko, Pityana and Ramphele, his laugh was loud and infectious, cutting through tensions. Thinking he could spare a couple of weeks, Mpumlwana came willingly to King William's Town. The weeks turned into months and years; in fact he never left.

A new group gathered, which flowered for a while in the tough climate of the Eastern Cape. Its members became some of Biko's most trusted comrades. When one person was restricted in one way or another their joint effort protected that person, and he or she went on working. Initially Biko was regional director of the BCP; Mapetla Mohapi came in to work for Saso, and Nohle Haya (who married Mohapi) was Steve's administrative assistant. Thoko Mbanjwa worked with Malusi (they later married). She, Biko and others did the research for the *Black Review* and Thoko edited the 1974–5 edition. Mxolisi Mvovo, married to Biko's sister Nobandile, worked as marketing officer for the home industries that the BCP was running. Nobandile worked with Thenjiwe Mtintso for the Border Council of Churches. Her work was closely connected to the BCP work, running self-help projects, bursary schemes and support programmes while Mtintso was field-worker for the Dependants' Conference, funding and working with ex-political prisoners in Dimbaza and elsewhere. Nomsa Williams did research for *Black Review,* and, later on, Peter Jones did the accounting of the BCP books.

The fact was that designation was irrelevant. Mtintso, for example, though she had had little writing experience, was assigned as journalist when Donald Woods gave Black Consciousness an opening on the newspaper he edited, the *Daily Dispatch.* Later, a regular column in the newspaper became Mapetla Mohapi's responsibility, in which the BC viewpoint was expressed. Its content was a group assignment, discussed and debated and even jointly written.

Mohapi later became administrator of the Zimele Trust Fund to aid ex-political prisoners, a totally different assignment. King William's Town soon had a research and publishing department running and a showroom to display clothes and leather-work made locally in home industry centres.

Several projects got under way throughout the country. A glance at the issues of *Black Review* of 1973–6 indicates the extent of what began to be researched and discussed, and underlines just how much there was to report. It attempted to be faithful to a wide range of aspects, thus making it today an invaluable source of information about youth, workers, education, theatre, writing, political organisations, political trials and so forth. *Black Review* had, as its companions, *Black Viewpoint* and *Black Perspectives*. Cottage industries, producing leather goods and cloth garments, were created in villages near King William's Town and, later, in Cape Town. The Zimele Trust Fund helped mainly ANC and PAC people, who were being released into the 'resettlement' areas where there was no employment; bursaries were also raised for their children. The Zanempilo Community Health Centre was officially opened in April 1975. Dr Mamphela Ramphele was its first medical doctor and came to live at the clinic. Training courses in leadership, which also conscientised blacks to their reality, continued throughout the country, particularly among the youth. Hierarchy was automatically discouraged. It was literally pointless and diminished the growth of what was possible. Apart from aiding the system, dominance by individuals would prevent the evolution of ideas. 'We must not create a leadership cult. We must centralize the people's attention onto the real message,' Biko said. Curiously the word 'democracy' was not part of the language; rather the word used was 'communal'. More and more people, who were themselves active elsewhere, dropped into 15a Leopold Street from all over the country.

Black Consciousness took root and grew in spite of the draconian restrictions of the 1970s, when each year claimed more banned, and more detentions were made, often under the ferocious Section 6 of the Terrorism Act. With no access to lawyers allowed, no certainty of being charged, detainees were often kept for months in prison in solitary confinement, taken away from their work for long periods of time. Almost everyone whose name is mentioned here suffered detention of one sort or another. Many left the country: Mafuna and Serote went to Botswana in 1974, around the time that the current Saso–BPC leadership was arrested for holding an illegal rally to celebrate the Frelimo victory in Mozambique. Others left later, many in the aftermath of the 1976 student uprising to join the armed wings of the ANC and PAC; some only returned from exile in 1990, after President De Klerk's declaration of 2 February, which put an end to apartheid.

Biko defined Black Consciousness as 'an attitude of mind and a way of life'. Its philosophy was to express 'group pride and the determination of the black to rise and attain the envisaged self'; its realisation was to recognise that 'the most potent weapon in the hands of the oppressor is the *mind* of the oppressed'; its methodology was to enable the evolution of ideas to flourish and thereby give a wider range of people the chance to voice opinions, even if some were inarticulate and hesitant at first. Those who lived and learnt through this method and understood it, became a nationwide community and took that rootedness within them into whatever area of the struggle they later found themselves. The influence of Black Consciousness stimulated and helped to change the nature of the major liberation movements with a surge of new thinking and energy. It is an integral part of that history, recognised at the time, though the nature of its contribution has not been sufficiently acknowledged.

In the context of the community which he helped to create, Biko was seen as one of the most selfless. He was consistently available to others in ways outlined earlier: his room at medical residence was everybody's room, his house in Natal was everybody's house, his mother's home in Ginsberg became the focal point until the Zanempilo Centre was created – a crucial asset in that time of banning and dislocation. Because of this, people were prevented from being isolated and went on functioning. Biko, too, could not have survived without the many others. His personality, however, broke the taboos of the time and had a freeing influence on those who worked with him. Instead of needing to consult him every day, they began to find it exhilarating to be independent, seeing him from time to time for sheer pleasure and for rejuvenation in defiance of the authoritarian State. Mpumlwana describes Biko as a visionary and an adventurer, being 'like the plough with virgin soil to till; but the field would not bear any fruit without all the other implements, including the seed and the rain'. Biko knew this. It would be an insult to separate him from the wholeness of the process. He also needed to be cared for, needed love. He sought it in other people as much as they sought it in him. In spite of the harsh realities he faced and dealt with, he had a softness and a gentle sensibility.

There were costs. Enormous dedication and extremely hard work were required. Ramphele remembers: 'I was on duty 24 hours a day, 7 days a week, 52 weeks of the year' at the clinic. This necessitated a submersion of individuality and sometimes the suppression of aspects of individual talent and growth.

'It became a duty to be tolerant and to listen; it was necessary to be able to accept criticism and act on it.' One of the drawbacks was that having experienced the support of the group and the circle, some found it difficult to adapt to other circumstances, especially when they went into exile.

For most, however, it was a nurturing ground for the potential within them that otherwise might not have been realised. Developing trust took its time but was rewarding and cost-effective in the end. Those who built it then have a particular bond, in spite of having taken different personal, political and professional roads.

On 19 October 1977, a month after Biko died, all the Black Consciousness organisations were banned and people further scattered through banishment and imprisonment. Out of anger over his death and in dedication to what he stood for, many of those who had worked with him refused to let things die. Ramphele, virtually single-handed, built a new clinic at Ithuseng, near Tzaneen, in the district to which she was banished; Mpumlwana continued his mediation work through the churches, preventing many a death in later years; Pityana went into exile and became a priest, later working for the Programme to Combat Racism in the international arena of the World Council of Churches; Thoko Mpumlwana stayed in King William's Town and expanded the Ginsberg Educational Trust to include the whole Border region – it became known as the Zingisa Educational Project. Nohle Mohapi joined Thoko and worked for Zingisa until 1990, when she began a new branch in Port Elizabeth, Khanyisa. Thenjiwe Mtintso, who suffered appalling treatment and torture in prison, went into exile and joined the armed struggle in MK. Later, she became the ANC's ambassador to Uganda. She remembers that 'When we built that community, around Steve, around King William's Town, it really made us. It really made the good parts of me. We were building together, we were fumbling along, starting so many things together, and that made us. And that created the political discipline that we think we have. If you simply look at that lot that came from King William's Town, then went to Lesotho – there were seven of us who went into exile in January 1979 – they were given responsibilities even when we had just joined the ANC. They were young people in their twenties – but quite mature, quite disciplined and very committed and serious. We worked like slaves. Work was not torture, it was part of your whole life.'

'King was my political home. The group began to be my political school. And Steve began to be my political mentor as a person. But [he] went further than that. He was my counsellor in my own private.life. He was a friend, he was a brother, he could actually be all these things, put together. I don't want to put him beyond being a human being. He had his faults, many of them, but one thing I liked about him was the care. Steve could read your mood, could take time to talk about your own life … He had this attraction for all of us I think. He was not an enigma – he was … I can't explain it, but I can only say that it was that attraction and that attachment and wanting to spend as much time as possible with Steve, whether in a political or social or informal context.'

Political strategy

The Black People's Convention (BPC) had been established in June 1972 to expand the work of Black Consciousness beyond the student and youth groups of Saso. At its first conference in December it debated two points of view: whether it was to be an umbrella, culturally orientated organisation acting as a parent body to all African organisations, or a direct political body through which blacks would realise their aspirations. Over the next two years it sought to find its feet despite continual harassment and banning of its leadership. In September 1974, in conjunction with Saso, rallies were planned in solidarity with the victory of Frelimo to mark the installation of Mozambique's new transitional government. The rallies in South Africa were banned the night before. It was decided, however, that the rally due to take place at Curries Fountain in Durban would go ahead. Biko himself was not in agreement with this. According to the *Black Review*, about five thousand people had gathered there. The police arrived, broke up the rally and arrested people on the spot. They then rounded up many others from the numerous offices of Saso, BPC, the Black Allied Workers' Union, and so on – all the Black Consciousness groupings, in fact. Those arrested were held under Section 6 (1) of the Terrorism Act, which allowed for indefinite detention, incommunicado. Seven months after the arrests, 13 people were charged in April 1975 under the Terrorism Act. By the time Biko gave evidence in May 1976, there were nine accused.

As Mpumlwana drove the newly released Mohapi from Pretoria to Natal in early 1975, they debated the role that BPC might now play. An idea grew that it should explore its potential as a catalyst for uniting the liberation movements for several different reasons: the logic that Black Consciousness should now develop from its psychological unity to a political unity; the fact that, in spite of the personal bannings, Saso and BPC still had mobility and continued to operate nationally on the ground; the recognition that the ANC and the PAC were the established political movements and that BPC would not act as a third force but would endeavour to create a national consciousness involving all the existing historical political movements against the common enemy. It was a delicate matter and, compared to the two banned Congresses, BPC was a fledgling organisation. The proposal would need to get a mandate. Nevertheless they were convinced, as Pityana asserts, 'that Black Consciousness provided a common programme, one with which the entire liberation [movement] could identify', that they had to assert that the stature and leadership of the ANC and PAC were unassailable. 'So, again and again, we acknowledged both the authority of the liberation organisations and the authentic leadership in prison or in exile.' Pityana explains that 'it was really the only basis on which the ANC or PAC militants could associate with Black Consciousness'.

The idea was discussed with Biko and others from different parts of the country. Influenced by developments in Zimbabwe of unity between Zanu and Zapu, BPC set out to test its bona fides with the banned PAC and ANC and also with other, smaller political groupings like the Unity Movement. Contact was made with known ANC and PAC supporters in the country, notably the lawyer Griffiths Mxenge and Robert Sobukwe respectively. The two were sympathetic to the idea. They in turn agreed to contact their underground organisations internally and externally. Confidence grew and BPC people travelled extensively. Biko also travelled when necessary.

Saso and BPC had good standing with other political groupings still functioning in South Africa. A joint project was being planned to protest against the apartheid government's policy to make the Transkei 'independent' in October 1976. This involved the Unity Movement and other groupings in the Western Cape, where some community programmes were also founded in common, and good personal links were formed. BPC felt that if practical united action was possible along these lines it would later help to build trust for the idea of a greater political unity.

The next BPC congress was held in King William's Town in December 1975, the same month in which Biko's new restriction orders prevented him from working for the Black Community Programmes. At the congress policy documents were proposed and debated. The idea was that these were to be used as working documents in the negotiations with the ANC and the PAC. However, most people at the congress knew nothing about these planned talks. In the political climate of the time the security risk was too great for the normal open discussion on such matters. This undemocratic approach must be acknowledged, but there did not seem to be any alternative. It had taken nearly a year of 'delicate shuttle diplomacy to persuade both the ANC and the PAC representatives to agree in principle to a joint meeting to explore the question of mutual co-operation,' Mpumlwana explained. The meeting, due to take place immediately after Christmas, involved not only banned people but also the banned organisations.

An economic policy document was written to avoid possible withdrawal of either PAC or ANC. It took its starting-point as 'Black communalism', described in *Black Review* as 'a modified version of the traditional African economic lifestyle which is geared to meet the demands of a highly industrialised and modern economy'. It gave considerable power to the State and local communities but avoided defining itself in Marxist terms or employing the classical class analysis. This document, as well as one on the vision of a future State, met with considerable criticism. Mafika Pascal Gwala (editor of the earlier *Black Review* of 1973) saw it as a 'reversal of development and history' and remembers how he quarrelled with Biko about it. At a further workshop in Mafeking in May 1976, he and others like Diliza Mji, Faith Matlaopane, Norman Dubazana and Nkosazana Dlamini felt that proposing far-reaching policy documents was no business of the BPC but the prerogative of the ANC and should involve the 'fleshing out' of the Freedom Charter, Mpumlwana reports. Such policies could smack of the beginnings of a third force rather than an attempt to find common ground.

All this was happening at just about the very moment that Biko was subpoenaed to give evidence in the Saso–BPC Trial. In the confined space of the court in Pretoria, the heart of apartheid's power-base, Biko chose his words carefully. 'We are advocating black communalism which is, in many ways, similar to African socialism. We are expropriating an essentially tribal background to accommodate what is an expanded economic concept now. We have got to accommodate industry. We have got to accommodate the whole relationship between industry and politics. But there is a certain plasticity in this interpretation precisely because no one has yet made an ultimate definition of it.' He proceeded to talk of bargaining and the importance of dialogue between themselves, who held this African socialist view, and those 'who hold dear a free enterprise system, and out of these two clearly the synthesis will come'. Although he was talking in apartheid's law courts – this can hardly be defined as a clear economic policy – Biko was also speaking to a broader audience. He now determined that two things were critical to his agenda: to better understand the nature of economic forces and to further pursue the growing debate about the validity of class analysis.

The nine charged under the Terrorism Act were mostly people he knew, some close friends. His task was to define Black Consciousness so that they might not be given severe sentences – the mandatory sentence for anyone charged under the Act was a minimum of five years. The case tested all of Biko's skills and was an example of his obvious eligibility for becoming a lawyer. He displayed the capacity to walk through a minefield of cross-examination without compromising himself or incriminating the accused. In the dock Biko often appeared to control the argument, either as the astute politician or the story-teller, the humourist or the teacher. In the expression of his answers lies the compassion for his country and its people.

Having accepted the conditions of participating in the due process of the law of the land, his first test was to assess the situation. The evidence led by David Soggot, assistant counsel for the defence, gave him the chance to state clearly what Black Consciousness was as well as inspire people once again with dignity and pride, defining Saso and BPC to be concerned with 'the whole development of the human being, in other words the black man discarding his own psychological oppression', he explained. Under cross-examination by both the defence and the State, he emphasised why the historical logic of Black Consciousness was blatantly obvious and reasonable. His assessment of Judge Boshoff was to draw him into dialogue. He answered his questions as if in a genuine debate, drawing the judge into some insights where the judge indicated

Biko in conversation with Richard L. Baltimore III, a US diplomat and political officer.

interest beyond the scope of the case, about one-party states in Africa, the meaning of democracy and the merits of the gold standard.

Biko did not treat the prosecutor in the same manner. This was more the cat-and-mouse game he had practised for so long with the Security Police. Almost immediately he made it clear that shoddy definitions and bullying tactics held no sway with him. He displayed his ease of intellect by redefining questions or words, using the very techniques he would expect a good lawyer to use, with skill and apparent confidence. He used humour and ironic references to whites to express the ironic nature of their society. There was a discussion of the meaning of the apartheid system. The definition flowed from 'the police' into 'institutionalised racism', with a graphic example of Biko having to use the 'white' toilet in the very building they were in and the marked display of racism he encountered as he did so, even though there was no 'black' one. And when asked whether he described himself as a freedom fighter, he immediately knew where that came from and challenged:

Biko: 'I did use the expression once to Security Police who wanted to know what my profession was, and I said I was a freedom fighter.'

Prosecutor: 'I think that was with tongue in cheek, not so?'

Biko: 'Well, it was making conversation, and if you have got to live with the Security Police on your neck all the time you have got to devise a way of talking to them, you know, and this is one of the ways. Generally, they understand in only one language.'

Those four days must have helped to restore any morale that might have been low amongst those who were charged; it would have revitalised the fearful and restored solidarity, and assured them that they were amongst those pushing forward the struggle. Reading the evidence today makes us forget the tense and dangerous circumstances under which it was given, makes it tempting to assume that this *was* Biko's own true testament and the 1976 expression of Black Consciousness. Partly it is, but there were terrible pitfalls that were set up, which Biko avoided in a remarkable way. The atmosphere was one of deliberate intimidation. The prosecutor constantly led arguments in which he attempted to connect Black Consciousness, and those charged, with the politics of the banned movements and their leaders. Biko was called at the very time that the BPC was embarking on its unifying role aimed at making contact with those banned organisations, and his genius lay in the way in which he kept many balls in the air at once, not compromising, not intimidating and yet maintaining the attention of the judge.

Not everything he said was exactly the way it was. In the feature film about Biko, *Cry Freedom*, the script-writer used the court record to elicit evidence that Black Consciousness was non-violent. This was not entirely true in reality. The policy of BPC was to explore the non-violent route, but many BC people were disillusioned with this approach and were leaving the country to follow the political logic of the armed struggle and join it. The atmosphere of the court was highly charged. Mandla Langa, another witness, feared for Biko's openness and obvious display of a superior intellect, feared his manner would do him harm: 'It was like war, really; you could feel the enmity.'

Members of the international world began to

recognise Black Consciousness, as articulated by Biko, as a key political voice in the country, whereas for most white South Africans, Biko's reply to the prosecutor's question probably sums it up:

Prosecutor: 'So you agree with me that the whites basically are afraid of Black Consciousness?'

Biko: 'I would say that the majority of whites are not even aware of Black Consciousness.'

Within a month of Biko's giving evidence in Pretoria, on 16 June 1976, a transforming political event occurred, the Soweto Uprising. The school children of Soweto came out onto the streets en masse, protesting against the imposition of Afrikaans as a medium of instruction. Dissatisfaction and restlessness had been brewing for some time against many aspects of the inferior Bantu Education system but this new regulation was the last straw. It mobilised into action a national peaceful protest. The retaliation was police bullets, which claimed the lives of hundreds of young people throughout the country. Reminiscent of Sharpeville, this had major implications both at home and abroad. Thousands of students crossed the border illegally to take up arms. Some joined MK, others the military wing of the PAC. Their full stories are only beginning to be told. The Soweto Uprising and its aftermath changed the face of South African politics, including Black Consciousness. Biko told me personally that no specific organisation could claim the uprising. 'It took us all by surprise,' he said. How much of it was spurred by eight years of Black Consciousness and its contact with youth organisations is yet to be fully assessed.

6

Choices and dilemmas

In spite of not having been in agreement with the decision to defy the ban on the Curries Fountain meeting, it must have been a relief for Biko to have performed his task well at the Saso–BPC Trial. When those in the trial had begun to be arrested in 1974, Biko expressed in a letter to Father Stubbs that he felt 'a strange kind of guilt'; he felt a responsibility that 'so many friends of mine have been arrested for activities in something I was most instrumental in starting', a lot of them 'blokes I spoke into the movement'. He comforts himself somewhat by saying that nobody knows why some of them were included and also that no trend in the movement warrants the 'terror act' being invoked. He then reminds himself that 'one does not think this way in political life, of course'. Casualties are expected and should be bargained for. 'An oppressive system often is illogical in the application of suppression', he wrote to Stubbs in a letter.

In the same letter Biko admitted that for himself the going had been 'tough under the present restrictions'. Again, he qualified this with his usual optimism and confidence: 'I am nowhere near despair and frustration but can understand only too well why some of our guys are.' He saw the positives in his life: 'a supportive and defensive township', 'reasonably fulfilling work' and 'I live with a very supportive family, one which is fully committed to my commitment if not to the cause itself'.

Biko seldom revealed his fears openly. Both his sister Nobandile and his colleague Thenjiwe Mtintso say that if banning did get him down, it never showed. Emotionally he took on the mantle of the father to his extended family. Once he had a job he became joint supporter with his elder sister Bukelwa in looking after his mother, insisting that she stop working. After the sudden and tragic death of Bukelwa of a heart attack, in his mother's house in September 1975, he and Ntsiki carried the responsibility. He also displayed a responsibility to everyone with whom he worked, including those he had worked with, now banned or banished.

It was only to the very few that he revealed doubts and his own inner misgivings. Father Stubbs was one of these people and the evenings he spent with David Russell, he wrote, 'were very good palliatives to the mental decay that so easily sets in'. To Ntsiki he expressed the expectation that she would be widowed before he was 30. When his frustration occasionally burst into uncontrolled rage, to the shock of those around him, because it was rare and so uncharacteristic, Ramphele was one of the few people who could calm him down and get him to go away to some quiet place. He shared many of his innermost thoughts with her as well.

He talks of his supportive family being committed 'to *my* commitment if not to the cause itself'. Biko was surrounded by women who loved and nurtured him, and Mamcethe, Ntsiki and Nobandile, his younger sister, complemented his life with their dedicated care. Women's inclusion by men in the 'just causes' to which they are dedicated has often assumed that those women will always perform the functional tasks in the preparation of food and drink, provide a safe base, love and comfort. With this goes also the assumed superiority of the man's intellect and choice of work, which is given time and space to be expressed. In spite of her key role as doctor in charge of the clinic, Ramphele also did her fair share of this kind of nurturing support for all the visitors who came to see Biko there. (He sometimes ate two meals, one there and one at his mother's home, and he put on weight.) However, women in the BC movement were aware that it was exploitative. Mtintso remembers that 'there was no way you could think of Steve making a cup of tea or whatever for himself'. She herself once refused to do so for him and met the consequences.

Biko did, indeed, expect this 'traditional' support, but he and others also assumed an equality of purpose and capability from the women who worked with them. Biko was filled with admiration after Mtintso had withstood very rough treatment and torture in prison. Mtintso comments wryly: 'We would have our revolts. They do want women to be political, to be active, to be everything, but they still need a complement of women who are subservient', and this was why (other) women were always brought into the *gumbas* 'to add glamour to the party'.

Ramphele was more and more an example who defied these traditional codes. In relation to Biko, not only had Ramphele become the professional doctor with a secure income, but he had long sounded out his ideas with her, and expressed his excitement while she helped him to remain consistent in the application of his ideas. She had been a constant sounding-board in his political thinking and this made a huge difference in the restricted environment of King William's Town. He could also unburden himself to her when necessary. Ramphele took little notice of his flirtation with other women, being confident in herself and of the depth of their own recognition of each other. After 101 days in prison – much of it in solitary confinement – at the end of 1976, with considerable time to think about his life, Biko came clean with some of these flirtations; she couldn't believe it and laughed and laughed. He admitted that the two of them seemed bound in a common destiny and he admitted that it was partly *that* that he had been trying to escape. She remembers him saying something like: 'I know we are two strong personalities and there is no way you are going to submit to me nor am I going to submit to you, so we have to negotiate our relationship.'

Ntsiki Biko understood his nature well, too, and accepted it in a different way. 'It needed somebody with strong convictions, or strong – I don't know whether to call it love for somebody – to stay with him. I doubt very much, even if I had left him, I am sure he would have married several times. I know he wouldn't have lasted in marriage. And I know he was very fond of his kids.' However, by early 1977, Ntsiki took her own independent stance. She began to look for another post, and when a job came up in mid-year at All Saints Hospital in Engcobo in the Transkei, she told Biko she intended to move away and set about filing for a divorce. No matter how much she challenged Biko, he did not change. His approach to her as his wife remained what is perhaps best described as traditional, with that expectation of a role-model wife who was supposed to understand and accept whatever her husband chose to do. Ntsiki loved Steve but circumstances went beyond her endurance. Particularly as his wife and, maybe one should add, as the daughter-in-law of Mamcethe, for whom Ntsiki had deep respect, there was the added difficulty of making personal demands against the powerful circumstances into which she had fallen: her husband was banned and deeply committed politically; people came to consult with him night and day; there was the necessity for her to have a job to survive, not only financially but also personally; the job was outside her husband's magisterial district; there was the knowledge that Steve was bound in with Mamphela, politically deeply committed to the work she was doing and all that surrounded her, including the powerful status which being a doctor carried in the community, especially as a woman; the fact that the clinic had become his logical political base. Ntsiki was not aggressive, did not expect to perform the undignified task of fighting for her committed rights as a wife, her inalienable rights as a married woman. They had talked through the things that upset her, constantly, and she had conceded a great deal regarding his work, 'but the relationship part was becoming too much,' she said. 'It was beyond my acceptance,' she said. Ntsiki never stopped loving Steve.

7

Detentions, banishment and international engagement

There was a crackdown in the King William's Town area. One month after the Soweto Uprising, on 15 July 1976, Mapetla Mohapi was arrested and detained at Kei Road police station under the Terrorism Act. He died in detention three weeks later on 5 August. This was a tremendous shock. It was alleged that he hanged himself with a pair of jeans. It was clear that he hadn't. The post-mortem was conducted by Dr R.B.R. Hawke, a pathologist, in the presence of two doctors, Dr Ramphele and Dr Msawuli, who were themselves then detained on 13 and 29 August respectively under the Internal Security Act. Biko was detained on 27 August, and Mvovo, Mpumlwana, Mbanjwa and Mtintso in the same month. Mohapi's widow, Nohle, ran the office for four months until they were all released in December, when Mtintso was banned to Johannesburg and

Mvovo to Dimbaza. In March 1977 Mpumlwana, now married to Thoko Mbanjwa, was held under Section 6 of the Terrorism Act for another four months. At the beginning of April, Father Stubbs was stopped by police on his way from Port Elizabeth airport to a local church where he was to preach on Good Friday; he was body-searched and ordered to strip, an indignity Biko thoroughly disapproved of.

In the same month, Ramphele was banished to the northern Transvaal. She was removed, suddenly and swiftly, from the BCP offices in Leopold Street by the police, only having time to grab her handbag, and driven over 1200 kilometres north. Within days of her arrival, having been told where she was to work in a particular hospital, she realised that the number on the warrant for her arrest and banishment did not coincide with her Reference Book. Even her name was spelt wrongly. She rang her lawyer, Raymond Tucker, who agreed this made her banning order null and void. Her young brother, Thomas, had just arrived to see her. 'All she said was, "Good! I'm glad you've come. Now we're off," bundled him into the car and drove the 200-odd miles to Johannesburg.' At 4 a.m. Ramphele and Father Stubbs left St Peter's Priory in Johannesburg and drove to the Zanempilo Centre, arriving twelve hours later. Great reunions, but only for ten days, before the system, slightly embarrassed, got its act together and banished her again for seven years. In those few, defiant days Hlumelo Biko was conceived, to be born after his father's death, miles away in Lenyenye, where Ramphele, having refused to work in the place assigned to her, began to establish the remarkable clinic of Ithuseng. After the long detentions of 1976 the State continued to break up and destroy the carefully established network all over the country by consistently removing people. Staff in the office and at the clinic went down to a minimum, the column in the *Dispatch* ceased. The signs were ominous and the State was menacing, but there was nothing to do except carry on.

Peter Jones, who was an activist in the Western Cape region of BPC in 1975–6, was asked by Biko to come and help manage the office in King William's Town. He had been part of a team, including Mpumlwana, Mvovo and Thandisizwe Mazibuko, who travelled widely to enlist support for the campaign to protest against the government's move to make the Transkei an 'independent' country. By now it was conceded by a growing political consensus that the Black Consciousness Movement was 'the least contentious' of the political organisations to attempt some kind of unity of focus for all the liberation movements in spite of the fact that the planned meeting between the banned organisations had had to be postponed

Biko (right) accompanied by Donald Woods (left), editor of the Daily Dispatch, *who gave the Black Consciousness Movement a column in his newspaper to put across its viewpoint.*

in December 1975. 'The relationship with anyone outside [the country] was based on the nature of the relationship we had with people inside the country,' says Jones. By 1977 these 'people were very close to us. There was no credibility problem. And because of Steve's quiet position he [was] the best placed to personally promote it.' In January 1977 Biko was appointed honorary president of BPC in order to provide him with the leadership identity necessary. Jones explains that he was 'more visible than a lot of other leadership within our organisation, not media visibility but a crucial kind of visibility'. It was decided that Biko should secure an invitation from abroad. In April, when Father Stubbs had delivered Ramphele back to the clinic, Biko asked him to procure some such invitation in the UK or Europe, which he did. Biko made the same request of Lein van den Bergh, a Dutch lawyer who, representing a Dutch funding agency, visited King William's Town around that time.

Representatives and diplomats of foreign countries, constantly on the look-out for personalities representing different opinion, began to consult Biko as someone who held the key to what was going on in the black world. This was partly the result of his performance in the Saso–BPC Trial but also because of the arrest of virtually all the leadership of the Black Consciousness Movement, including himself.

In December 1976 Senator Dick Clark, chairman of the US Senate Sub-committee for Africa, who was attending a conference in Lesotho, applied to the government to see Biko while he was still in detention. Biko was released just before they were due to meet. Mpumlwana reports that immediately Biko knew this, he 'sent word to us in prison that he was out, was seeing Dick Clark and asked, "What should I say to him?" That evening we battered our way at a statement, which we smuggled out early to influence his presentation.' Even under these circumstances there was consultation. Biko presented Clark with a memorandum entitled 'American Policy Towards Azania'. After a polite preamble the memorandum pointed out that although words had been abundant by US politicians in condemning apartheid, 'very little by way of constructive action has been taken to apply concerted pressure on [the] minority white South African regime'. Clark made a press statement after meeting Biko, saying that 'I talk to Vorster [the South African prime minister] when I want to find out what the Government are thinking. I have talked to Mr Biko to find out what blacks are thinking'.

Soon after this Biko was invited to the US, under the auspices of the USA-SA Leadership Exchange Programme, but he refused, explaining that he would only accept such an invitation when 'America had given proof of a radically changed policy towards South Africa'. In most of the liberation movements, the US was considered 'imperialist', a country whose foreign policy towards other countries preferred 'economic stability' under an oppressive regime, rather than supporting a people's struggle for democratic human rights which might invoke radical political views in order to attain them. Biko expressed to Donald Woods how Western countries merely 'slapped the wrist' of the South African government but 'maintained their diplomatic and economic links that helped to bolster the regime'.

As repression closed in on the Black Consciousness Movement, contact with the outside world became more and more important. It was, metaphorically, the only 'court of appeal' in the increasingly dangerous atmosphere in South Africa, where the judiciary was virtually castrated by the legislature. Biko immediately recognised the usefulness of diplomacy amidst the growing danger that surrounded him and his colleagues. More and more people were dying in detention. The strategy was to inform the outside world as precisely as possible about the nature of that detention and the necessity to act against the South African government.

In a recorded interview with an American businessman, probably made around January 1977, Biko speaks about what detainees were up against. It was after Mtintso had been beaten up and tortured, and Biko was very angry. 'When I went into jail, my friend [Mohapi] had just died. He was the 24th person to die in jail since 1973. When I came out, they were talking about number 27. And this is happening increasingly now, because of the frustration the police are having. They want quick information. Now, there's an extent to which a person can absorb beating without revealing information. But sometimes it so happens that, in fact, the person being assaulted doesn't [have the information]. And they simply go on and on with a towel around your neck saying "Speak" – and you say nothing – "Speak" – you say nothing – and the bloody brutes are not trained well enough to realise when enough is enough. So by the time they release the towel you have been dead for a couple of minutes.'

In January 1977 he met with Bruce Haigh, second secretary in the Australian Embassy. As they drove out to a quiet and secluded place of Biko's choice (to avoid the bugged BCP office), Biko expressed interest in the current political and economic situation in Australia, stating that he looked to that country and others, like Scandinavia, Britain and the US, for some answer as to how the process of democracy would deal with the demands of an evolving technocratic society.

Biko led the discussion throughout, covering a wide range of topics, giving Haigh important information

– for example, what he felt were the reasons for his own detention. Haigh reports: 'They [the police] were trying to find out how many students had fled to Botswana and Swaziland and what they were doing there. They knew very little and he had been unable to help them.' Biko then gave Haigh the real information: that several thousand students had fled since the Soweto and country-wide uprising, and that 'lines of communication had been established between them and the students still in South Africa', and that Biko believed demonstrations would now be smaller in order to avoid loss of life; his expectation was 'that in future small groups of two or three people would probably start using explosive devices against selected buildings and government installations'.

Further, it was his opinion that 'the students felt that as activists they had a legitimate claim to lead the protest movement', that 'the ANC and PAC were building up their organisations within South Africa once again, but this was only after the students had created the pre-conditions for their return and re-organisation'. The youth who went into exile helped inject new energy and life into the liberation movements, informing and influencing them directly in assessing the thrust of the current political climate. Some went in the hopes of further education but most went to take up arms.

Biko treated Haigh as an intelligent ally, giving him

In 1976–7, foreign diplomats, academics and journalists sought out Biko. Bruce Haigh, Second Secretary in the Australian Embassy, realised he was in danger and asked his government to 'Please protect Biko'.

careful political information throughout the visit. Haigh himself was strongly aware of the danger surrounding Biko. In his very last entry in his report he wrote an appeal to his government: 'Please protect Biko.'

In these last recorded interviews with Biko – notably by foreigners – the strategy was to get information out fast. It was important to understand each interviewer and Biko assessed what would be the best information for each one of them so that it could be carried as far as possible to the right quarters. In these interviews we are again struck by Biko's astute understanding of the people he is meeting and of the situation at hand, in spite of the banning to isolate him. In August 1977, speaking to the American Committee on Africa, he explained that BPC's 'line' was to explore the non-violent road within the country, but that there was also the view 'that the present Nationalist government can only be unseated by people operating a military wing'. His own opinion was that 'in the end there is going to be a totality of effect of a number of change-agencies operating in South Africa'. He would also like to see fewer groups: 'I would like to see groups like ANC, PAC and the Black Consciousness Movement deciding to form one liberation group and it is only, I think, when black people are so dedicated and so united in their cause that we can effect the greatest result.'

8

Arrest

When he spoke those words, Biko had long since set out on that course. Only a few days later, he left for Cape Town on 17 August, once again breaking his banning order. Through Peter Jones he had a long-standing plan to meet with various people there. There was also a need to settle some possible dissension within the BC ranks. Biko hoped as well to meet Neville Alexander, who, having once been a member of the Unity Movement in the 1960s, now represented an important political grouping in the Western Cape. Alexander had served ten years in prison on Robben Island with the major ANC and PAC leadership and had been banned and house-arrested on his release in 1975. He was an articulate exponent of the class analysis and had considerable influence in this regard. Although Biko wished to see Alexander for other reasons, he had expressed interest in his political views and might have hoped for a stimulating debate as well.

But the times were very risky, and before he left King William's Town, Alexander had said he would not be able to see him. 'I had not been mandated to see him and could not get such a mandate in time,' he later said. This message was not communicated to Biko, who only discovered it on arrival.

This attitude was difficult for Biko to accept, and he waited for three hours outside Alexander's house while Fikile Bam, a comrade who had also served ten years on Robben Island with Alexander, was brought in to discuss whether he might change his mind. This was a high-risk operation for all three men: Alexander was banned and house-arrested and under constant surveillance; Bam had been banished to the Transkei homeland and had to get special permission to enter the Republic of South Africa; and Biko could have been recognised at any moment.

Jones intimates the growing unease they felt. 'A few other things happened in the course of that night. We just felt that we were not in control of the situation. There were too many shadows around us.' In the very early morning they decided to 'disappear'. Driving back to the Eastern Cape, Jones recalls that Biko obviously had things on his mind. 'For the first time we were actually talking personal things. We were going through his life, his marriage and stuff, and I was going through my girl-friend at the time

– I wasn't married – and my aspirations, and so on. What hit me was I couldn't recall any other time when we spoke with so much clarity.' Nearing the end of the long journey, round about 10.20 p.m., Jones was driving into Grahamstown. Biko had a tape-recorder on his lap and they were listening to a tape. Both were lighthearted and relaxed. As they came round the bend they ran into a roadblock of uniformed policemen and 'a number of plainclothes men I realised were Security Police'.

When requested to open the boot, Jones had difficulties because it was not a car he knew. While waiting for this to be executed, one of the plainclothes officers asked Jones where he was going. 'East London,' he replied. Then the man looked at Jones and said: 'Jy gaan seker vir ou Biko sien' (You're no doubt going to visit that chap Biko). Peter showed no reaction and said: 'Who's Biko?'

Impatient with the intransigent boot, the same plainclothes officer, Lt. Oosthuizen, 'suggested I should follow them to the charge office where the car could be searched,' Jones remembers. At the charge office, having identified Peter Jones by his wallet, the police then asked Biko what his name was. '"I am Bantu Stephen Biko," he replied. For several moments there was absolute silence with police just looking at both of us. "Biko?" Oosthuizen asked. "No, Bantu

131

Stephen Biko," said Steve, giving the correct Xhosa pronunciation to the *b*'s.'

Next morning they were 'viciously handcuffed' and removed to Port Elizabeth to the sixth floor of the Security Police headquarters at the Sanlam Building, handcuffed by one hand to the bars, then photographed, taken back outside, 'separated by two squads of police who surrounded each of us … I was in front and Steve a few paces behind me.

'My entourage stopped at a Kombi [van] and I was told to enter and lie face down on the floor between the seats. I turned to look at Steve who just passed and called his name out loud. He stopped to look at me and called my name and we stared, smiling a greeting, which was interrupted when I was slapped violently into the Kombi. That was the last time I was to see my close comrade ever – alive or dead.'

Peter Jones was held for 533 days without trial. He was finally released in February 1979. For the first 25 days during which time Biko was also held, he tells us what happened to him in the hands of the Port Elizabeth police, the same team which interrogated Biko. 'The first session lasted for more than twenty hours. I left my cell at about 22.00 hours [on 24 August] and was brought back at about 18.00 hours the following night. … We drove at high speed to Sanlam Building … Immediately I entered the room I was held by several police while one of my hands was freed and my clothes taken off. I was made to sit naked on a chair with my left hand chained with the handcuff to the chair. Snyman and Siebert occupied chairs at desks respectively to the left and right of me.

'On the desk in front of Siebert was a length of green hosepipe. I was able to look right into the hole of the pipe and noticed that the hole was filled – with what, I cannot say, but it was something metallic.' General questions followed. 'Then suddenly they focused on the trip Biko and I had been on ... I repeated my original story that I had gone down to Cape Town to attend to a newly established project there (a clothing factory) and that Steve's presence was incidental and unplanned with no other intention than giving him an "outing" ... Siebert suddenly jumped up and hit me with the hosepipe across my face and chest and arms, and then returned to his seat ... Siebert told me they knew we had been in Port Elizabeth, that we had dropped pamphlets and that we had seen or met some people with whom we distributed these pamphlets. After some time of following this trend I told the police that in fact we had been in Cape Town to have discussions with our BPC men there.' Jones was given pen and paper to write two statements: his political history and the story of the trip. This did not satisfy Siebert, who ordered two policemen to put him *op die stene*

Marthinus Prins, inquest magistrate.

Dr Ivor Lang, the first doctor to examine Biko.

B. de V. Pickard, counsel for the doctors.

Capt. D.P. Siebert, one of Biko's and Jones's interrogators.

(on the bricks). Soon after this Siebert re-entered, accompanied now by Snyman, Nieuwoudt, Marx and Beneke.

After some resistance Jones was forced onto two small pieces of brick. 'Two chairs (heavy steel ones) were placed one on top of the other (the one upside down), and both Beneke and Nieuwoudt had to lift these until I could hold them high above my head. Siebert told me that should the chairs lower or fall I would "get it". I told him it was impossible to hold. I was already experiencing cramps in my legs.' Questions followed on Jones's involvement in BPC and BCP. Jones lowered the chairs to his shoulders. They were taken away and he was again chained to the chair and, again, the subject of the pamphlets and Port Elizabeth came up. When he repeatedly said he knew nothing, he was again placed on the bricks.

'Snyman started calling me names and calling me a liar. He got up from his chair and kicked me on the left leg. I stumbled and the chairs came tumbling down, one hitting him on the head and the other landing on Siebert's desk … I was taken from the bricks, on which I had by now spent several hours. Siebert got up and asked me when I was going to stop lying, and started to deliver heavy blows with both hands (open) to my face. I grabbed both his hands and pulled him down towards me. I told him that the treatment was unnecessary as I was answering their questions. Siebert, who is smaller than me, told me to let go of him, and did I want to fight? Two fist blows followed, delivered by Nieuwoudt and Beneke … these two grabbed my arms.

'Siebert removed his watch and rolled up his sleeves. For a very long time he slapped my face with both hands (open) continuously and without pause. I remained silent, felt my senses dimming gradually to the stage where I could with a detachedness just feel the blows going through my head while I looked straight into Siebert's eyes.

'Just behind Siebert was a mirror hanging on the wall and I could see my face … amazed that my face could assume such dimensions. Another "lip" was forming, blood from my mouth and nose, mixed with spittle, dribbled down my face onto my chest … Marx and Snyman now stood to the left and right of Siebert, facing me, and Nieuwoudt started delivering fast and heavy blows to my head with the hosepipe, which was excruciating in the kind of shocks it sent through my body.

'Then Beneke started hitting me with his fist in my stomach and I started to stumble. Marx got a boot to my right leg as a warning to stand still. Beneke left and from a drawer of a filing cabinet took another hosepipe, black this time. Marx shouted: "Give him both – black power and green power!" Beneke took up his position again, on my left, and from then on he and Nieuwoudt hit me mainly on the head with hosepipes while Siebert carried on smacking my face. Snyman and Marx delivered kicks to my shins whenever I moved out of the way.

'Every time I tried to defend my head with my hands the pipes would move to the back, the kidney area, or attack the hands. I found it impossible to cope with all the immense pain and I turned and faced the wall and, closing my eyes, began hoping for oblivion, which never came, as blows rained down on my head and back.'

This interrogation of Jones took place on 24–25 August. According to the evidence at the inquest and amnesty hearing, Biko's interrogation began on 6 September in the same small, isolated room. For the eighteen days prior to this he was apparently held naked, in solitary confinement, in the Walmer police cells. There, 'he was deprived even of the negligible rights he had as a section 6 detainee. He was not taken out for a minimum period of exercise … not allowed to purchase food … not allowed proper washing facilities.' We do not know whether Biko was interrogated like Jones before 6 September, but on that day he was told to put on a shirt and trousers and taken to the Sanlam Building. In Room 619 Biko was interrogated by precisely the same team under the leadership of Maj. Harold Snyman: Warrant-Officer Ruben Marx, Det.-Sgt. Nieuwoudt, Capt. Siebert and Warrant-Officer Beneke.

Peter Jones lived to tell his story. Bantu Stephen Biko did not.

At the inquest into Biko's death – Jones was still in prison – Lt.-Col. Goosen, head of the Eastern Cape Security Police, said: 'Major Snyman reported to me that Mr Biko had become very aggressive and had thrown a chair at him and had attacked Warrant-Officer Beneke with his fists. A measure of force had to be used to subdue him so that he could be handcuffed again. I immediately visited Mr Biko. He was sitting on the sleeping mat with his hands handcuffed and the leg-irons fixed to an iron grille. I noticed a swelling on his upper lip. There was a wild expression in his eyes. I talked to him but he ignored me.'

We still do not know the whole truth of what happened to cause the fatal injury in Biko's case. In spite of the opportunity to tell the truth to the TRC in 1998, none of the five men who simultaneously assaulted him has owned up to the actual blow or blows to the head, or to causing his head to hit the wall, which left major brain injuries and changed Biko from a perfectly healthy human being into a physical and mental wreck in a very short space of time. At the inquest into his death in detention, Advocate Sydney

Kentridge put the Security Police 'on trial' in so far as was humanly possible in a State that ensured police protection by law. Callousness, lies and brutality were in evidence day after day.

The doctors who supposedly examined Biko displayed a pathetic weakness in the face of the Security Police – a chronic lack of care or compassion. They disgraced their profession. At a point when Biko's brain was damaged, when he was deranged to the extent of no longer being in control of his bodily functions, Col. Goosen cynically described his condition as that of 'shamming'. 'Neither I nor any of my colleagues, nor the doctors saw any external injuries'. Goosen then put in the order for Biko to be transported, naked, in the back of a Landrover for the distance of hundreds of kilometres from Port Elizabeth to Pretoria. This was conceded to by Dr Benjamin Tucker, Chief District Surgeon, Port Elizabeth, who at the inquest averred: 'I didn't know that in this particular situation one could over-ride the decisions made by a responsible police officer.'

In the judgment, Magistrate Marthinus Prins pronounced that 'on the available evidence the death cannot be attributed to any act or omission amounting to a criminal offence on the part of any person'.

Whether Biko defended himself with the chair on which he sat without permission – if this was not

Sydney Kentridge, Ernie Wentzel and George Bizos at the inquest.

itself a fabrication – or whether what happened to Jones happened in more or less the same way to Biko is not of major significance in the face of the violence of his death. South Africa's security laws enabled policemen to be unaccountable. Protection of the most irresponsible policemen ensured that no court could condemn them. Beatings and other torture resulting in deaths were safely, symbiotically, locked into a protective conspiracy between police witnesses and the State. What happened in Room 619 happened countless times. The security laws allowed detainees to be held in terror without any protection. Doctors, magistrates and others were willing to compromise the integrity of their professions in the shadow of these laws, thus making the law a mockery but ensuring that it was played out as if it was not. Perjury was a matter of course.

A supreme arrogance persisted into and throughout the 1980s. At the time of Biko's death, the Minister of Police, Jimmy Kruger, was at a National Party congress in the Transvaal. In his first announcement reporting it, he said that Biko had died 'following a hunger strike', adding that 'Biko's death leaves me cold'. A quip from the audience by one Christoffel Venter responded that Mr Kruger was so democratic that he allowed detainees 'the democratic right to starve themselves to death'.

Twelve years later Father Aelred Stubbs cast his mind back on Biko and the preservation of the innermost person in that extreme situation. 'I am trying to work from my knowledge of Steve and my knowledge of his deepest values and instincts,' he said. 'I am sure that there was a kind of inner fortress of integrity that he would not suffer to be violated.' He knew that Biko was prudent with a sense of self-preservation and, although only a stupid person would have no fear, Biko had conquered fear in an intelligent way. 'He had a much greater fear of betraying himself than a fear of physical violence even to the point of death. He had conquered fear by his inner conviction of his outer undefeatability if he was prepared to give everything. That kind of quality grows with exercise.

A deep instinct; very very deep, absolutely rooted in the roots of his culture. Steve grasped the essential goodness of what was there and worked from that, allowed that to work within him, always broadening it as his own horizons did.'

9

A life still to be 'dug out'

Barney Pityana was still in prison on 12 September, the day Biko died, and was not told of his death. That night he had a dream. He dreamt that he had 'this enormous discussion with Steve where he was saying, more or less, "I am leaving. You must look after my children", and I saying, "You know it's not *my* business to look after your children – you must do something responsible."' Biko went on, insisting in a friendly sort of way, until Pityana reluctantly agreed that, all right, if he *had* to go somewhere, he, Barney, would look after his children. The next day Pityana was allowed to have a shower, something not allowed before, and 'this white boy was reading the paper and I managed to see in his paper a statement by Kruger. I would otherwise never have known and then suddenly this sort of funny discussion I was having in the middle of the night came back. I was in a very very lonely state in that cell. I was absolutely distraught, angry – much more, [I was] almost suicidal.'

'It was the fire – the fire went out.' Ramphele looked out of the window as she spoke. 'When Thenjiwe phoned me on 13 September I was in hospital. When I heard, everything went dead. I literally wondered if I could walk across that room, if I could survive physically. Everything was dead.' Mamphela Ramphele was banished, isolated in Lenyenye, far in the north, in hospital, trying to save the life of her unborn child – Biko's child.

Biko's funeral took place on 25 September at the King William's Town stadium. Oxen drew the coffin until it was lifted and held shoulder-high by his comrades, an impulsive gesture which was to become the hallmark of the many funerals of comrades to come. The only visible presence of the State was one lone soldier seen on a tower high above the crowd. Otherwise the police were not present. But, as Mafika Gwala explains, they were present elsewhere: 'Most Natalians missed [Steve's funeral], the result of police action in turning the cars and buses carrying mourners back on the Transkeian borders ... [but] I did not miss the symbolism that such burial carried ... Those who have attended the funerals of all those who have died in detention must have gone to these funerals with an inner understanding that a scratch on a black man is a scratch on every black man. And that death in detention at one centre is death in detention all over the country … When we heard that Steve was dead many of us must have said, deep down in our minds, if the time must come, let it begin now.'

Biko knew that it *had* already begun. The youth of Soweto, of Natal, of the Eastern Cape, of Langa, Nyanga and Guguletu in the Western Cape – the youth of the whole country – had understood that. As Biko explained, 'The dramatic thing about the bravery of these youths is that they have now discovered, or accepted, what everybody knows: that the bond between life and death is absolute. You are either alive and proud or you are dead, and when you're dead you can't care anyway. And your method of death can itself be a politicising thing; so you die in the riots. For a hell of a lot of them, in fact, there's really nothing to lose – almost literally; given the kind of situations that they come from. So if you can overcome personal fear for death, which is a highly irrational thing, you know, then you're on your way.'

Biko's mother understood this too. 'In truth he was not my child. He was the son of the people. I have come to understand that I must comfort myself and accept that truth: that this child was not my child. Moreover, there are many children of other people who have gone before Steve. When a battle is fought, not all the soldiers come back home. It is God's will in which this

At Biko's funeral: wife Ntsiki, son Samora and mother Mamcethe.

whole thing happened. After such a long time *bube ubomi bakhe busombiwa* [his life is still being dug out]. Accepting that, I have a humble view of myself as a person from whom he comes.'

Biko foresaw his death in the nature of what he was doing, and he was prepared to die. Thus, along with

146

many others, he became a martyr in the struggle for freedom in South Africa. He fulfilled his own concept of obedience to God, which was, as he explained, 'at the heart of the conviction of most selfless revolutionaries, a call to men of conscience to offer themselves, and sometimes their lives, for the eradication of evil'.

Biko was only 30 when he died. In the slow and tortuous manner of his death he endured a kind of crucifixion, chained and unable to move, his feet in irons hooked into the wall; with people always watching. After suffering a blow to his head so severe that it gradually undermined his mind and consciousness, his capacity to function as a human being, he was, after five days, declared fit enough to be driven, naked, in the back of a Landrover 1133 kilometres overnight. Yet, on arrival in Pretoria, he was still not dead. He died alone shortly thereafter.

In his own words, his 'method of death' was, indeed, 'a politicising thing'. It woke up the world to the true nature of apartheid and accelerated commitment to fight for change in all forms inside and outside South Africa. Dying young, Biko left a life of such promise in the air, so to speak. Of those who knew him at the time, Mpumlwana said: 'We all each individually experienced it. You can't replace the catalyst that he was. None of the other people we related to were *that* to you – and yet he didn't get to you. He was best at not making you grovel with gratitude. We couldn't have another Steve.' Donald Woods, in his exuberant style, said that he was simply 'the greatest man I ever met'. Lein van den Bergh, a Dutch lawyer, who was a member of the Resistance in the Second World War and experienced imprisonment at Dachau, met him only once and saw in him the qualities of a man whom he would expect to become 'the leader of the government'. Some of his political critics then were less impressed. In the *African Communist*, for example, Biko was accused of 'being a "liberal", an idealist, insufficiently anti-capitalist, a pacifist, and lacking any understanding of the mass struggle', but in a recent radio interview Kedibone Molema said, 'Biko took people out of an ethnic identity and allowed us to have another. That was a galvanising thing,'

Biko had a clear insight into the psychological aspect of the oppression of his time which had resulted in momentary political impotence. As politics was racialised by apartheid, the movement was called *Black* Consciousness. His message was simple and clear: *Do not be a part of your oppression.* It was a crucial intervention, a fresh, youthful and distinctive voice that mobilised people when all the major political opposition was banned, their leaders in exile or in jail. It provided a new, vital, unifying element giving to the ANC, as Wally Serote said, 'oxygen and new life, which the movement desperately needed'.

Black Consciousness worked with consensus decision-making. It instilled independent thinking, self-reliance, fearlessness and dignity. It had a wider concept, black power, which connected both with the emergence of Africa's independence from colonial rule and with that other significant struggle for black liberation in the US. In South Africa, Biko and his contemporaries broke the stunned silence of their time.

The refusal of a new generation of young blacks to be subservient or humiliated, even in the face of death, changed the nature of the struggle. Biko himself lived and died by this truth. Just before his death he was on the verge of meeting the leadership of the ANC and the PAC in exile to discuss the possibility of a unifying force. Biko's leadership and the role of Black Consciousness have yet to be truly estimated and cannot be tucked away into a small paragraph of history. A key catalyst of transformation, Biko's generation inspired a culture of fearlessness. This was made more resolute when the government responded by killing hundreds of young people in the Soweto Uprising and its aftermath. Fearlessness was sustained throughout the 1980s, when apartheid's policies manifested a mounting violence with secret assassination squads and army troops with teargas and bullets daily in the townships. Protests on the ground escalated whilst a growing number of MK guerrillas – including many from the BC movement – infiltrated South Africa country-wide. The situation was becoming ungovernable and evolving into an undeclared civil war. Funerals of black cadres were vast and became political platforms for further resistance. The flags of the banned organisations re-emerged in the carrying of the coffins. It was, indeed, 'the awakening of the people' whose sheer numbers made the politicians move. Black South Africans never felt inferior again.

Black Consciousness held the value of not wanting to be rich at the expense of the poor. 'If we have a mere change of those in government positions, what is likely to happen is that black people will continue to be poor and you will get a few blacks filtering through the so-called bourgeoisie and our society will be run almost as of yesterday,' Biko said. How, then, would he view the current, growing gap between rich and poor in South Africa's new democracy? What would he do about it? What would he think of the cult of materialism and greed? Or the jousting for status, money and position amongst South Africa's new elite – anathema to his style of leadership – with its failure of delivery to the majority, still imprisoned by the legacy of apartheid, whose youth continue to be undereducated and unemployed? In 1972 Biko ironically suggested that if the apartheid government was smart and wanted to be re-accepted into the world, it should create a black minority elite, a wealthy middle class, and retain the vast majority in poverty to provide a pool for cheap labour from which to draw. Is this close to the scenario emerging today in South Africa after the intense struggle and supreme sacrifices made for freedom and equality? Where would Biko stand today? Would he be inside the tent or outside? What is certain is that, first, he would interrogate the facts as to what exactly is going on in all spheres of South African life. If true to form, he would ensure this information was followed with country-wide debate around the issues; this would be led by consensus leadership and result in informed action.

One feature of South African society that would undoubtedly claim his attention and dismay him is the prevalence of violence and abuse of women and children, South Africa's rape statistics being one of the highest in the world – a stark negation of 'group pride and the determination to rise and attain the envisaged self'. 'Do not be a part of your own oppression'. His words sustain well into the 21st century. They determine analysis of the individual self and the call for action. In the 1970s Biko's words often spoke directly to 'the black *man*'. In 2011 the substitution of 'black *women*' might aptly apply to these words of his: 'The essence is the realisation by *women* of the need to rally together with *her sisters* around the cause of their oppression and to operate as a group to rid themselves of the shackles that bind them to perpetual servitude. It is based on a self-examination which has ultimately led them to believe that by seeking to run away from themselves, they are insulting the intelligence of whoever created them *women*. The philosophy of Black Consciousness expresses group pride and the determination … to rise and attain the envisaged self.'

Biko's spirit is far from dead. Nor is it confined to the movement he inspired but extends to the wider truths he held and expressed through the liberating experience of recognising that Black Consciousness could be the transforming agent of his time. It will always be true that 'the most potent weapon in the hands of the oppressor is the mind of the oppressed'. Biko's life is still 'to be dug out' as a transforming agent wherever oppression is rife. His life-force was an antidote to pessimism. Biko was essentially *living*. He would thoroughly object to becoming a myth locked away in the room of a museum or in the rigid, inappropriate statue of himself in East London. With his intellect, huge presence and raucous laughter and the 'no bullshit thing', he liberated the spirit of those he met. He used every opportunity available, weighing up a situation precisely and swiftly, seeing its limits as much as its potential, understanding how to make it work for the common purpose, knowing nothing was perfect and that you had to work very hard to transform anything. He worked with the potential of individuals, often locked away within them, knowing that without the recognition and subsequent growth of that potential a nation could not function fully. He worked with whoever came his way. He was not elitist in spite of having commenced initially as a student leader from a university. There was no time to waste and he knew he had to sacrifice his formal education. Later, he sensed that he would have to sacrifice his life. The strength of his particular style of leadership stemmed from his capacity for astute political insight coupled with his faith and recognition that anyone could grow, learn, and participate and lead once challenged with meaningful ideas, and from this could emerge a meaningful life.

Biko's perception and energy freed people to take their destiny into their own hands. How they will continue to draw on his insight and legacy is up to new generations. But his memory would best be served by the growth of a broader consciousness that remains wary of mindless authority, that recognises that ideas are strengthened through consensus decision-making, which has the capacity to be persuaded by a majority vote, even if it sometimes seems inappropriate, and, simultaneously, has the ability to then work with that decision, ensuring its soundness.

Bibliography

Apartheid Museum, *Biko: The Quest for a True Humanity – Exhibition*

Arnold, Millard, *Steve Biko: No Fears Expressed* (Skotaville, 1987)

Bernstein, Hilda, *No. 46: Steve Biko* (IDAF, 1978)

Biko, Steve, *I Write What I Like* (Heinemann, 1988)

Bizos, George, *No One to Blame* (David Philip, 1998)

Black Review, 1972–1976

Erikson, E.H., *Identity* (Faber & Faber, 1968)

Gerhart, G.M., *Black Power in South Africa* (University of California Press, 1978)

Freire, Paulo, *The Pedagogy of the Oppressed* (Penguin, 1972)

Lodge, T., *Black Politics in South Africa since 1945* (Ravan, 1983)

Marx, A.W., *Lessons of the Struggle* (Oxford University Press, 1992)

Mngxitama, A. et al., *Biko Lives* (Macmillan, 1998)

Moore, Basil, *Black Theology* (C. Hurst, 1973)

Mutloatse, Mothobi, *Reconstruction* (Skotaville, 1981)

New Republic, January 1978

Pityana, Barney et al., *Bounds of Possibility* (Zed Books and David Philip, 1991)

Ramphele, Mamphela, *A Life* (David Philip, 1995)

Van Wyk, C., *Steve Biko*, Freedom Fighters Series (Maskew Miller Longman, 2003)

Wilson, Monica and Leonard Thompson, *The Oxford History of South Africa*, 2 vols. (Oxford, 1969, 1971)

Woods, Donald, *Biko* (Henry Holt, 1987)

Notes taken by Pamela Reynolds at the Biko Amnesty Hearing, 30 March 1998

Interview with Steve Biko by Gail Gerhart (1972)

Interviews with Lindy Wilson:

Neville Alexander (Hogsback, 1991)

Nokuzola 'Mamcethe' Biko (Ginsberg, 1989)

Nobandile Biko (Mdantsane, 1990)

Nontsikelelo (Ntsiki) Biko (1990)

Neville Curtis (Harare, 1990)

Mafika Gwala (London, 1989)

Anne Hope (Cape Town, 1991)

Bennie A. Khoapa (Roma, Lesotho, 1990)

Mandla Langa (London, 1989)

Bokwe Mafuna (Paris, 1989)

Malusi Mpumlwana (Grahamstown, 1990)

Thenjiwe Mtintso (Harare, 1990)

Nyameko Barney Pityana (Geneva, 1989)

Dimza Pityana (Geneva, 1989)

Mamphela Ramphele (Cape Town, 1989)

David Russell (Grahamstown, 1990)

Mongane Wally Serote (Harare, 1990)

Aelred Stubbs (Sunderland, 1989)

Francis Wilson (Cape Town, 1991)

Videos and DVDs:

Biko Inquest (102 mins), 1984: dramatisation of the transcripts of the Biko Inquest by John Blair and Norman Fenton (with Albert Finney as Sydney Kentridge)

Biko: Breaking the Silence (52 mins), 1987

Biko: The Spirit Lives (67 mins), 1988

Steve Biko: Journey of the Spirit (52 mins), 1997

Steve Bantu Biko: Beacon of Hope (53 mins), 1999

Index

African National Congress (ANC) 15, 26, 48, 94, 96, 101–4, 110, 127
African socialism 16
Alexander, Neville 129
Bam, Fikile 130
bannings (March 1973) 77–8, 84–91; (August 1976) 118–24; (October 1977) 98
Beneke, Warrant-Officer 135–8
Biko, Alice Nokuzola 'Mamcethe' (mother) 18–3, 79, 114, 145
Biko, Bantu Stephen (Steve): birth and early years 18–29; schooling 22–7; as university student 30–56; medical studies 16, 28–9, 57, 70; law studies 16, 28, 105–8; president of Saso 36; joins BCP in Durban 57; banning to Ginsberg (1973) 77–9, 84–91, 113; further restriction (1975) 103; gives evidence at Saso-BPC Trial 105–10; imprisonment (1976) 75, 115–16; honorary president of BPC 122; arrest (August 1977) and death (12 September 1977) 11–13, 129–42; funeral 144–5; inquest 13; gift of leadership 14, 41–2, 44, 49, 52–3, 87–7; generosity of intimacy 15, 61–5, 114–15; love and marriage 65–75; socialising 49–51, 91–2; writing 40–1; reading 45–8; on religion 16, 24–6, 75, 80–3
Biko, Bukelwa (sister) 19, 113
Biko, Hlumelo 72, 120
Biko, Khaya (brother) 19, 23, 27
Biko, Mzingaye (father) 18–19
Biko, Nkosinathi 72
Biko, Nobandile (sister) 19, 20–1, 93, 113, 114
Biko, Nontsikelelo (Ntsiki) (wife) 67, 68–72, 113, 114, 116–17
Biko, Samora 72
Bizos, George 13
Black communalism 104
Black Community Programmes (BCP) 57, 60, 77, 79, 85
Black Consciousness 14, 17, 41–3, 62, 77, 87, 91, 95, 96, 101, 106, 148–54
Black Panthers 48
Black People's Convention (BPC) 85, 100–3, 105–10, 128
Black Power 32, 42
Black Review 60, 91, 93, 94, 101, 104
Black Workers' Project 52, 101

Boshoff, Judge 107
Cape Town 41, 52, 80, 94, 129, 133
Charles Morgan Primary School 22
Christianity 24, 26, 75, 81–3
Church, the 16, 24–5, 39, 82–3
Civil Rights movement 42
Clark, Dick 123
communism 27
Cone, James 47
conscientisation 32, 57, 95
Cooper, Saths 45, 46, 59, 78
Cry Freedom 109
Curtis, Neville 39, 61
Daily Dispatch 91, 93, 120
Dimbaza 80, 93, 119
Dlamini, Nkosazana 104
Durban 39, 52, 57, 68, 77, 91, 92, 101
Erikson, Eric 54
Fanon, Frantz 47
fearlessness 84, 88, 90, 141, 149
Forbes Grant Secondary School 22
Freedom Charter 104
Freire, Paulo 42, 59
Frelimo 95, 100
Freud, Sigmund 54, 65
Gabriel, Peter 11
General Student Council (GSC) 46, 48
Gerhart, Gail 76
Ginsberg 19, 20, 57, 70, 79, 88, 97
Goosen, P.J. 13, 138
Grey Hospital 20
Gwala, Mafika 46, 104, 144
Haigh, Bruce 125–6
Hope, Anne 59
Internal Security Act 118
Issel, Johnny 59
'I Write What I Like' 40, 71
Ithuseng Clinic 98
Johannesburg 50, 52, 59, 78, 88, 118, 119

Jones, Peter 93, 120–2, 129–38
Kentridge, Sydney 138–9
Khoapa, Bennie 57, 60, 83
King William's Town 19, 20, 67, 78, 85, 103, 118
King, Martin Luther 47, 64
Koka, Drake 78
Kruger, Jimmy 141, 143
Langa, Mandla 45, 46, 47, 109
liberalism 24, 28, 39
Lovedale Institution 23, 33
Mafuna, Bokwe 50, 51, 59, 78, 95
Malcolm X 47
Mandela, Nelson 27
Marcuse, Herbert 46
Marx, Ruben 135–8
Marxism 16
Matshoba, Deborah 59
Mbanjwa, Thoko 93, 99, 118, 119
Mji, Diliza 104
Modisane, Jerry 59, 78
Mohapi, Mapetla 93, 101, 118, 125
Mohapi, Nohle 69, 93, 99
Moodley, Strini 45, 46, 59, 78
Mphahlele, Eskia 46
Mpumlwana, Malusi 15, 40, 85, 86, 92, 97, 98, 101, 118, 120, 123
Mtintso, Thenjiwe 88, 93, 99, 114, 115, 118, 125
Mvovo, Mxolisi 93, 118, 120
Mxenge, Griffiths 102
National Union of South African Students (Nusas) 30–1, 39
Ndebele, Njabulo 46
Négritude 42
Nengwekhulu, Harry R. 57, 78
Nieuwoudt, Gideon 12, 13, 135
non-racism 31
non-violence 109
non-white 40
Ntwasa, Stanley 50
oppression 14, 54–5

159

Pan Africanist Congress (PAC) 15, 23, 26, 94, 96, 101–4, 110, 127

Pityana, Barney 16, 33, 34, 35, 40, 41, 46, 48, 59, 63, 68, 78, 88, 98, 143–4

Pityana, Nosidima (Dimza) 62, 68

Poqo 27

Port Elizabeth 11, 19, 33, 52, 78, 88, 99, 119, 132, 135, 139

Prins, Marthinus 139

Rambally, Asha 45

Ramphele, Mamphela 45, 62–3, 67, 71–2, 94–5, 97–8, 114, 115–17, 118, 119–20, 144

Rand Daily Mail 50

Rhodes University 30–1

Rivonia Trial 27, 86–7

Russell, David 25, 79–81, 84, 88, 113

Sartre, Jean-Paul 46

SASO *Newsletter* 40

Saso-BPC Trial 16, 105–10, 122

Security Police 11, 64, 79, 83, 85, 107–8, 132–41

Serote, Mongane Wally 46, 50, 64, 95

Sharpeville 26, 110

Shezi, Mthuli 59

Sibisi, Charles 45

Siebert, Daantjie 12, 133–7

Snyman, Harold 12, 133–7

Sobukwe, Robert 102

Soggot, David 106

South African State 43, 77, 97, 120

South African Students' Organisation (Saso) 36–8, 39, 40,
43, 50, 71, 85, 100, 105–10

Soweto Uprising 110, 118, 149

St Francis College 24, 25

St Matthew's Hospital 19

Stubbs, Aelred 24–5, 52, 65, 73, 88, 112, 113, 119, 122, 141

Terrorism Act 95, 101, 106, 118, 119

Theatre Council of Natal 45

trade unions 15, 52–3

Transkei 103, 120, 130

Truth and Reconciliation Commission (TRC) 12, 13

Tucker, Benjamin 139

Tucker, Raymond 119

Umkhonto weSizwe (MK) 27, 99, 110

Unity Movement 103, 129

University Christian Movement (UCM) 34, 35, 39, 50

University of Fort Hare 33, 34, 35

University of Natal Medical School (UNNE) 28–9, 30, 45

University of South Africa (Unisa) 19, 60

University of the North (Turfloop) 36

Van den Bergh, Lein 122, 148

Verwoerd, H.F. 56

Vorster, B.J. 123

Woods, Donald 89, 93, 124, 148

Zanempilo Community Health Centre 67, 73, 94, 119

Zimele Trust Fund 94